D0856817

ADVENTURES OF ISAAC KNIGHT— INDIAN CAPTIVE

A True Story of the Northwest Territory for Young and Old Americans

by KEN McCUTCHAN

Greenwich Book Publishers
New York, N. Y.

A Reproduction by UNIGRAPHIC, INC.
1401 North Fares Avenue
Evansville, Indiana 47711
Nineteen Hundred Seventy Five

First Edition

Chapter 1

Isaac sat on the bank and watched the sun sink into the dark mass of forest on the opposite side of the river. In the last minute the big red disc literally dropped out of sight; then the long fingers of cloud that stretched across the sky turned orange and pink and made pretty colored reflections in the water.

The river was wide, and it moved lazily as if it too were tired of the day. Birds were doing their last errands among the fresh, green brush along the bank. Somewhere in the thicket a mocking bird sang an evening song to his mate on her new nest.

It was April and the long cold winter had gone. Isaac dreamed of the bright, warm days of summer that lay ahead. Soon it would be time to plant the potatoes and the corn. Soon it would be swimming weather, and he looked forward to the good times he would have in the river splashing in the cool water and romping with his friends and brothers on the soft, oozy sand bars. Sometimes there would be flat boats passing, loaded with new people and their belongings—new people from wonderful places far across the mountains called New York and Pennsylvania that father often spoke about. Isaac felt he was going to like this new home much better than the old one.

Almost as soon as the red ball of the sun was gone, the chill of the night came on like a damp, cold breath that rose up out of the ground and drifted in from off the river. He wrapped his arms tighter around his knees and watched the sky colors fade and the thin silver circle of a new moon come out in the sky where the sunset had been.

"Is—aac! Is—aac! Come to supper!" It was his mother calling.

Isaac's nose caught the salty odor of side meat frying. He jumped to his feet and scampered up the path between the big sycamore trees to the little clearing where the cabin stood. When he bounded through the door the younger children were already at the table dipping their spoons into their bowls of steaming, freshly cooked mush in milk.

The Knight family had just arrived at this new home on the Kentucky banks of the Ohio River. Previously, they had lived along the Green River, fifty miles upstream from where it empties into the Ohio. There the Green runs dark and narrow and deep. In places, the big trees leaned out from the opposite banks until they seemed nearly to clasp branches across the stream.

Life had not been easy there. The forest was thick, and the rocky hill soil was not too fertile. It took hard work to make crops grow. Then, too, there was always the danger of unfriendly Indians roaming the wilderness around them. Here on the Red Banks of the Ohio the soil was rich and already there were several cabins close by, almost enough to make a little village. There would be more safety here, as well as neighborly hands to help with the clearing and the planting and the harvest.

Isaac's father thought he had made a good business deal in buying the property. The cabin was sturdy, and even the small piece of land which was already cleared had produced one good crop of corn. It seemed an ideal location. "Life will be much better for all of us here on the Red Banks," he said.

However, moving to the new place had not been a simple task. Father and the two older boys, John and Joshua, worked all the month of March building a big raft with logs cut during the winter. Upon the raft they built a pen for the sow and her litter of new pigs, and a coop for the chickens and the geese. Toward the front they set up a canvas tent-like shelter to protect the family in case bad weather came up during the trip, and the rest of the space was left for piling the household goods. At first they had considered building a second raft to carry the two cows and the calf and the yoke of field oxen and the five goats, but on second thought Mr. Knight decided it would be better to drive the animals overland along the river bank. This task of course fell to Isaac and his brothers.

Finally, when everything was loaded and secured the family set out. It was the second day of April, 1793. Mr. Knight served as the boatman and guided the raft, keeping it always as close as possible to the shore where the boys were prodding the drowsy cattle along. This strange land-and-water caravan moved slowly. The undergrowth along the river bank was so thick in places that it was difficult sometimes to keep the cattle moving at all. They were always stopping to munch the tender young grass that was beginning to green up in the sunny spots, or chew off a branch that had tender new buds. Since the family also owned two horses, the boys sometimes rode, Isaac behind one or the other of his brothers. But when the going was easier and the forest more open, they would all walk, kicking up the dry last-winter's leaves. Sometimes they amused themselves by tossing pebbles over the river bank to hear them plunk into the water and see the rings of ripples spread out from where they sank.

At night the raft was tied to the river bank. The cows and the goats were milked, and all the animals were tethered nearby. After the evening meal sleep came to everyone quickly, but as a precaution the guns and powder horns were always kept within easy reach. Fortunately, the weapons were never needed, and the nights and days passed uneventfully, until the fifth day. It was then, when the party was less than a day's journey from the mouth of Green River, that something happened which was to affect Isaac directly in the months and years to follow.

It was a quiet, sunny morning, warm for April. The forest sent up the new green smell of spring. The cattle behaved well and the raft moved smoothly in a steady slow current. It was the kind of morning that makes one feel all good inside, the kind of day that makes one feel the world is truly a wonderful place to live in without evil or unhappiness or misery for any living creature. Isaac trotted along happily through the spring forest for several hours. Then, as the morning wore on, he climbed up onto one of the horses to ride behind his brother John.

Toward noon the boys suddenly saw a spot of unbroken sunshine through the trees ahead. This could mean but one thing—a settler's clearing. As they came into the open space, sure enough, set well back from the river was a neat, new cabin. The door and windows were tightly closed and no one stirred about, so the boys first thought the place was deserted. The cattle spread out among the stumps and began to munch the new grass which was much nicer here in the open sunshine than on the shaded and leaf-covered forest floor. The boys climbed down from their horses, and with the curiosity of all boys sensing the possibility of adventure, they began to explore. Joshua pointed out the fresh, clean chips and the bright edged ax at the wood pile.

"They can't have been away for long," he remarked.

"Maybe they have gone into the forest this morning to hunt meat," suggested Isaac.

"No matter," said John. "This is not our property and no affair of ours. We'd better get the cattle on the move or the raft will be away ahead of us and father will be angry."

Isaac couldn't resist taking just one peek in at the window, but just as he came up to the side of the house the door was flung back and a woman with a baby in her arms rushed out into the full sunshine. Her eyes were swollen and red, and tears were streaking down her white face.

"Thank God you are white men!" she cried "Thank God you've come—oh, thank God!"

Isaac, John, and Joshua were all so startled and frightened they would have turned tail and run if they had not been momentarily petrified in their tracks.

"When I heard your noise outside I thought they had come back. Oh, thank God!" she moaned and clutched the whimpering baby closer.

10

The three boys stood wide-eyed and open-mouthed.

"Who, ma'am?" was all John was able to stammer.

"Those beasts—those filthy savages who killed my husband. All morning long I've been afraid they'd come back and burn the house down over me and my children. Thank God it is you!" The woman buried her face against the child in her arms and broke into sobs so violent that her whole body trembled.

"Isaac, be quick. Run to the river bank and call to father. I think we're needed here." It was big brother John who had collected his wits enough to give the order, and Isaac did not hesitate to do as he was told.

In a very short time the raft was secured to a stout tree and the whole Knight family climbed up the bank to the clearing. There in the warm April noontime, the poor woman whose name was Kathleen Downs related the story of the frightful hours she had spent since dawn, the same hours that had seemed so serene to the Knight family as they moved along the river and through the forest only a few miles away. She told how she and her husband had arisen early, filled with plans for the new day. As soon as he was dressed he had picked up the pails and set out to get water from the spring in the edge of the woods behind the house.

"I remember he was whistling when he went up the path. He was in real good spirits this morning," she said, with big tears streaking down her cheeks. "I had just stirred up the fire and was getting ready to start our breakfast when I heard a shot. At first I thought it was him shooting a squirrel or something to surprise me with for breakfast. He was a great one for doing things like that—always doing little things to surprise me. And then I saw the rifle leaning there against the wall. Then I knew it wasn't him that shot. I ran to the back window, and I saw them—Indians running all over the place in the bushes back by the spring, but I couldn't see my man nowhere. Then I knew it right away. It was them who had shot him."

"Oh, you poor soul!" Mrs. Knight tried to comfort her.

"Could you tell how many there were?" asked Mr. Knight.

11

"Maybe six or seven, maybe eight. I'm not sure. They were running all around. All at once they set up a whoop that would freeze the blood . . . and then they held it up . . . and danced up and down laughing and yelling." She burst into hysterical sobs. "Oh God in heaven, it was horrible. I saw it happen once before. I know what they do to a white man."

Mrs. Knight put her protective arms around the trembling woman and pressed her head to her shoulder.

"There, there, dear. Try to hold yourself together. It's a terrible thing that's happened, but it's a blessing they didn't hurt the little one."

"Oh, I thank God for that," sobbed Mrs. Downs. "I thought for sure they would come to the house and try to break in, or set it afire and burn it down over our heads. I barred the door and windows and waited . . . and prayed they wouldn't hurt the children. I didn't care about myself. I just prayed for the children."

"And they didn't come around the house at all?"

"No, after awhile they just left and went away into the woods."

"That's how it is with those stinking savages," said Mr. Knight. "You never know where they are, or what they're going to do. It'll be a great day for the settlers when we can get this territory cleared of them."

"I thought sure they would come back later," continued Mrs. Downs. "I sat there behind the door all the morning with the rifle in my hands. When I heard the noise outside a bit ago, the noise of your lads here and the cattle, I was sure it was them. Oh, but thank God it was you, kind friends." And she burst again into uncontrolled weeping. "But my man is dead . . . dead . . .!"

"Come, my dear," said Mrs. Knight gently. "Let's go into the house and I'll help you put a kettle on. My menfolks will see what's to be done outside."

The women started slowly up the path, but as they came near the cabin, Mrs. Downs, as if suddenly remembering, broke away from Mrs. Knight's comforting arm and turned to face her, barring the path.

"No—!" she cried. "No! I can't let you go into my house. My boy Robert is in there. He's sick with the smallpox."

Isaac would not soon forget the scene at the spring. Mr. Downs had been shot and cruelly scalped by the red men, as the woman had said. There was nothing they could do except give the poor man a Christian burial. First they dug a grave on the hillside in the edge of the forest beneath the spreading branches of an old dogwood tree that was almost ready to flower. Mrs. Downs brought one of her best blankets from the house to wrap him in, for there were no proper boards at hand to build a coffin. Isaac's mother said a prayer as the body was let down into the ground, asking God to receive the good man's soul, and to watch over and protect the dear wife and the two fatherless children left behind, not forgetting to beg the kind Lord to heal the little sick one who was not able to come and stand at his father's graveside. Mr. Knight then read from the Holy Book: "I am the resurrection and the life; he that believeth in me, though he were dead, yet shall he live; and whosoever liveth and believeth in me shall never die, but have everlasting life."

After that, Mrs. Knight led the weeping widow away from the grave and the hole was filled. Upon the new mound of earth the boys laid large flat slabs of stone which they carried from the river bank. Finally it was done. That evening, after rounding up their livestock, the Knights returned to their raft, but not until they had begged Mrs. Downs to travel with them the next day.

"We can't bear to leave you here alone in the wilderness," pleaded Mrs. Knight.

But the woman would not consent to go with them. "In the first place my Robert is much too sick to travel," she argued. "And in the second place, I don't want to expose you good people any more to his smallpox. You already have been very kind. I shall never forget you, for I don't know what I'd have done if the good Lord hadn't sent you to me when he did. There is one more thing you can do," she continued, "if you will be so kind. When you come to the place where the Green River empties into the Ohio, which is less than a day's journey from here, find my brother and tell him what has happened. I'll be all right until he gets here, for I know that as soon as he has word of my condition he'll come at once. Then he can decide for me what I must do."

And so it was settled. The next morning at dawn the Knights resumed their journey, and by nightfall they had delivered the message. Travelling was easier when they came into the Ohio, and it took them only two days to reach the Red Banks. The rest of the journey was uneventful.

All these things Isaac thought about that evening as he ate his supper. The events of the week already seemed months away, although some of them had happened only yesterday. It was his mother's voice that brought him back to the present.

"Isaac is very tired, aren't you, son? You haven't said a word all through supper. This has been a hard trip for all of us, and we'll all sleep well in our new home tonight, I wager."

"Yes, I think we're all a little the worse for the wear," said Father. "But a good night's sleep will take care of that."

Pushing back his empty plate and turning to John and Joshua, he said, "First thing tomorrow morning we'd better build a pen to put the sow and her young ones in or she'll be traipsin' off into the forest and get herself lost, or the pigs eaten up. And Isaac . . ."

"Yes Father?"

"How would you like to take a little trip across the river tomorrow?"

"Oh could I? I'd like that very much."

"I was talking with neighbor Sprinkle this afternoon. He tells me that there are sloughs on the other side where cane grows. The tender young shoots at this time of year will make good feed for our stock. Sprinkle is sending his boys over in the morning. He said you could go along in the boat and help

14

them. Whatever the lot of you brings back we'll divide."

Isaac was overjoyed. The great river had fascinated him from the very first moment he had seen it, so crossing to the other side would be a wonderful trip. He was so delighted at the prospects that when he finally crawled between the blankets that night his last thoughts were of the fun he would have tomorrow.

Chapter 2

When the big red sun peeped over the edge of the east next morning, it looked upon a world all wet and silver with dew. The night had been cold, but not cold enough for frost. A thin veil of white mist lay on the breast of the river. It would be another lovely day.

As the old speckled rooster crowed his loudest greeting to the new morning, Isaac awoke with the happy realization that this was the day. He pulled his hands from beneath the quilts and rubbed his eyes. Beside him his brothers were still burrowed from head to heels in the covers, but downstairs there were soft sounds, and he knew that his father was up and dressing to go out and look after the animals.

He lay for a minute or two and gazed up at the yellow undersides of the clapboards on the roof over his head. A wasp sailed by and disappeared through a crack beneath the eaves. Isaac was not a boy to lie long in bed, especially on a morning such as this, when he was looking forward to the excursion across the river. He threw back the covers and sat up. The attic roof was too low to stand under, so he sat there on his pallet and pulled on his trousers and boots and jacket, and then crawled to the hole where he could let himself down into the main room of the cabin. As he climbed down the peg ladder he saw that his mother was already busy around the fireplace.

"Good morning, son," she called out. "Didn't you sleep well? You're such an early bird."

"Sure Mother, I slept real well," he replied as he bounded over to give her a good morning peck on the cheek. "But you know Father said I could go across the river today with the Sprinkle boys to cut the cane sprouts for the cattle. I was just thinking maybe they'd like to make an early start."

"Oh, I hardly think they'll be leaving so soon," she said as she bent down to adjust the logs in the fireplace. "Land sakes alive, you'd all be drowned in dew wading around in a cane brake this early in the morning.

"Here, you work the bellows for me," she said, standing upright again and wiping her hands on the underside of her great blue calico apron. "After you get a good blaze going you can go wash yourself for breakfast."

Of course Isaac knew that his mother was right, but he couldn't help being impatient. He thought breakfast would never be ready. His brothers were sleepyheads and his father seemed to stay much too long out of doors.

When finally everybody was gathered at the table and grace was said, he attacked his plate like a starving puppy and was all finished before the others were half through. Tucking the last piece of corn pone into his pocket, he sprang from the table and was out the door in a flash with his goodbye left trailing behind him.

"My goodness, that young 'un's in a mighty big hurry this morning," his mother said.

John remarked that he never seemed to be in such a rush when he had to take the cows to herd.

"Well, that's different," said father, laughing. "He looks on that as work, but this trip across the river is more of a lark. Those boys will have themselves a time, and we sure need some good fresh feed for the cattle—the cows especially. The old brown cow looks kind of poor, and she's way down in her milk. That long trip afoot has been hard on her."

16

When Isaac got down to the river bank he was still much too early. But the sun was beginning to climb up the sky and he knew that before long it would begin to burn the dew away. When the other boys finally came there were four of them. Peter Sprinkle was the oldest, a big fellow, almost a man—seventeen years old. Already he had hair on his face, and Isaac looked at him with the admiration of a younger boy who wanted desperately to grow up. Peter was tall and brown and sinewy, with a shock of curly, black hair. He carried a rifle and a powder horn, which was further proof that he was not a boy any longer. It was obvious that Peter Sprinkle would be in command of the expedition, and Isaac thought he would not mind in the least taking orders from him. There also was Peter's brother, George Sprinkle. George was around twelve years old. He was dark like his brother, but not nearly so tall and handsome. As a matter of fact, George was rather on the short side. Two other boys were with them. They were introduced as the Upp brothers, John and Jacob. John was nine and Jacob was only seven. Both had bright, orange-red hair and freckles. At first Isaac thought they had come down to the river only to watch, so it was with certain disdain that he learned they were going along too. His private thoughts were that children shouldn't be allowed to go on such a trip. They would only be in the way. After all, it was a work assignment, not a picnic.

Anyway, all five boys climbed into the wide, clumsy, flat-bottomed boat and pushed off. The Sprinkles, because it was their father's boat, worked the oars. The river was smooth, and it reflected the spring blue sky like a broad mirror. Only the wake of the boat disturbed the shimmery surface, leaving a long trailing scar on the water. Peter explained that to arrive on the other shore at a point exactly opposite the settlement it was necessary to direct the boat to a point considerably upstream. This point was marked for them by a big, old, white-barked sycamore tree. If they headed toward that tree until they reached midstream, Peter said, the river's current would carry the boat back, so that without too much hard rowing they would eventually arrive at the spot where he wanted to land.

As the shore drifted farther and farther behind them, Isaac began to realize for the first time just how big a river the Ohio really was. His heart began to beat with the excitement of adventure, for this was the first time he had ever been on such a vast stretch of water. The boat seemed very small and insecure when the shores were so far away, but he was not afraid for he had learned to swim a long time ago when they lived by the Green River.

The Sprinkle boys rowed with a firm, steady stroke. Boating was not new to them. They had lived on the Red Banks for a long time and they crossed the river often, sometimes for the cane and sometimes with their father to hunt possums and coons in the bottom lands.

The river sparkled in the morning sun. Once or twice a fish broke the smooth surface with a little splash when it flopped up to grab some unsuspecting insect that had come to rest on the water's surface. Isaac could feel the force of the current pushing against the boat, and he wondered what lay at the river's end—where they would go if they just let the boat be carried away. He had heard the older folks speak of New Orleans, but he had no idea how far away it was, how long it would take to get there, or what it was like. He had been born and reared among the trees in the forest and he had never seen a city.

"But I shall go there some day," he promised himself. "This very river will take me there."

He suddenly returned from his dream to realize that the other shore had come very near. As he looked back across the river the trees on the Kentucky side looked small. They were pale yellow-green in their first new leaves of Spring, and above them hung a blue haze of smoke from their cabins' chimneys.

The boat came to a jarring stop when the bottom ground into the sand bar. Peter jumped out first and ordered all hands to follow and help drag the craft to the solid dry sand.

"This is the life," thought Isaac. For a quick moment he

remembered to be thankful that he hadn't been given the job of herding the cows that day.

The boys were all out on the sand bar in an instant. As soon as the boat was drawn up they started having fun romping on the hard-packed brown beach, digging for shells and unusual pebbles which they showed to one another with pride before they cached them away in their pockets.

"Come on now. Let's let the playing go. We'll cut the cane first, and then if there's time we'll dig for some mussels before we go home." This was Peter Sprinkle taking command again.

Peter had the rifle and powder horn slung on his shoulder and two long wide-bladed knives in his hand. He passed one of the knives to his brother George. "Let's go," he said. He was the first to enter the first fringe of bushes, chopping away the vines and bothersome branches ahead of him. The others followed at his heels in single file. "My brother and I will take the first turn with the knives," he called back over his shoulder. "You other boys can carry the arm loads of cuttings back to the boat—and mind you spread them out evenly. This won't take long if everybody pitches in and keeps moving."

They pushed their way for about a hundred yards through the undergrowth over a sort of ridge that served as a river bank. The vegetation was extremely dense, and the trees carried vines high into their branches so that the forest was almost like a tropical jungle. Then the land became very low and marshy again, and there among the tall yellow stalks of the last year's growth were the fresh green cane sprouts they had come after. Peter took his rifle from his shoulder and carefully leaned it against the black trunk of a big, old cypress tree. He and his brother entered the swamp and started cutting the young, green cane. The other three boys began to collect the cuttings in their arms.

Isaac never knew exactly how it happened, or where they came from. He was stooping over to pick up a handful of the sprouts when all of a sudden he felt strong arms lock around

19

him, pinning his own to his sides so that he dropped the green cane he had just collected. At first he thought it was a playful antic of one of his companions, but in a flash the cruel reality struck him. The cane brake was alive with Indians. Before he could cry out a warning one of the savages leaped past him in an attempt to grab Peter, who was a few paces farther ahead. Peter turned at that instant, and Isaac saw the gleam of his knife blade as he took one wide swing at the approaching Indian. The blade missed its mark for a killing blow, but it grazed the shoulder of the savage, who let out a howl and grasped the wound with his hand as the bright red blood began to flow. Peter dashed past him in an attempt to reach the tree where the rifle stood, but before he could grasp it a shot sang out that echoed and re-echoed through the forest. The boy pitched forward and fell on his face. For one instant he seemed to half rise and stretch his arm toward the gun, but it was only a feeble effort, for he crumpled and was dead.

Isaac did not know what happened next. He knew that he cried out and that he put every ounce of his strength into one desperate effort to break away from his captor, but even though he kicked and struggled he finally realized that it was no use. The strong arms had lifted him completely off the ground, and he was merely thrashing his legs about helplessly in mid-air. Once he tried to bite the arm that held him so tightly. This got him nothing but a sharp cuff on the side of the head and a change of the hold—one arm around his middle and the other around his neck so tight it nearly choked him.

By this time he saw that two of the Indians were kneeling over the body of Peter Sprinkle. Suddenly, with a wild whoop, they leaped into the air. In one's hand was a mass of curly black hair. The other clutched a dripping red knife. Isaac was dazed with fright. His brain was spinning, and he was sick in his stomach. He could hear George Sprinkle screaming out against the savages who had just killed and scalped his brother, and he realized that George, like himself, was being held by the strong arms of another red man.

It all happened very quickly. The Indians, no doubt afraid

that the gun shot might attract attention to what they had done, were eager to get away from the place as quickly as possible. Isaac's feet and hands were bound with raw hide thongs, and he was tossed over his captor's shoulder like a sack of cornmeal. The other boys were treated in a like manner. Then, gathering their belongings, as well as the gun that Peter Sprinkle had left and the wide knives that had been used to cut the cane, the Indians set out single file through the forest in a trot.

Isaac's body bounced up and down on his captor's shoulder, the shoulder bone driving deeper into his stomach with every jolt. He thought he would soon vomit. Branches and briars lashed his face as the flight led deeper into the thick undergrowth of the low land.

After what seemed a very long time he realized that they were at last on the slope of a hill. The forest was more open now without the tangled vines they had passed through at first. He noticed that the Indians were growing tired and were slowing their pace. Perspiration was streaming down the back of the man who was carrying him. He knew he was getting heavy, and the frightening thought flashed through his mind that rather than have to carry him further the Indian might kill him to be rid of the burden.

Finally the party stopped. Isaac was tossed to the ground. They all dropped down to rest. For the first time since the beginning of the terrifying experience, he had a chance to look about him and actually see what kind of creatures these were that held him and his companions captive. There were eight Indians in the group. They were not all the same, this he could see at a glance. Although he didn't learn their tribal identification until later, six were Potowatamies and two were Kickapoos. His friends, like himself, were bound hand and foot. The Indians had been careful that they were not placed near one another.

Suddenly Isaac realized that there were only three white boys, including himself. There should have been four. Jacob Upp was not among them. He called out to the others and asked if they knew what had happened to the little red-haired boy; but no one had seen him in the excitement. Had he crept away unnoticed and escaped or had he, like Peter Sprinkle, met a crueler fate?

Isaac reckoned by the sun that they had been travelling in a northerly direction. The ground had risen considerably and he could look over the miles of tree tops in the bottom lands through which they had just passed and see glimpses of the wide river far away.

The Indians spoke little among themselves. They appeared to be young braves that had been on a war party. The one whose shoulder had been cut seemed much concerned about his wound. His face was drawn and fierce looking. After studying them all Isaac decided that his captor looked as good as any of them. It was obvious that the spoils of the expedition were being divided. Some had guns, some had knives from the cane brake, and each boy, likewise, seemed to be the sole property of the man who had first grabbed him.

When the rest period was over the Indians stood up and prepared to leave. Isaac's captor looked down at him, and then with a flourish, drew from his belt a bright knife which he brandished over his head.

"Please don't kill me!" cried Isaac.

The Indian bared his white teeth in a broad, mocking grin. Then, with two quick slashes of the knife, he cut the thongs from the boy's wrists and ankles.

"You walk," he grunted in English.

And so the flight continued. Isaac and George Sprinkle and John Upp took places in the single file among the Indians, Isaac directly in front of his captor so that he could be given a sharp poke in the back whenever his feet lagged.

All day they walked or ran, still going in a northerly direction. It was the longest day Isaac could ever remember. They did not stop for food or water, and his mouth became dry and parched with thirst. His empty stomach pained him.

His feet grew heavier and heavier. Now and then he would tear off a twig of sassafrass and chew it as they trotted on and on. This seemed, sometimes, to ease the hunger and the thirst —and then again it seemed to make them worse.

As the afternoon dragged by, the sun hid behind grey clouds and the wind grew more chill. Finally John Upp could go no further. He stumbled, caught himself up, stumbled again, and fell. His captor kicked him and threatened him with his tomahawk, but when he saw that the boy really did not have the strength to stand any more, he picked him up and set him on his shoulders. Isaac felt that he, himself, would not last much longer.

As dusk approached they came upon a small creek, almost hidden away among the low hanging boughs of the forest. Just as they reached the stream's edge a small bear that had been there for his evening drink leaped away into the brush. Two of the Indians gave chase and brought the animal down in no time.

With food and water at hand and night almost upon them, the party halted. Isaac wondered, had it not been for the bear, would they have continued the march? He felt he could not have withstood any more.

They all knelt down to drink. Then, as the boys fell back on the thick layer of brown leaves, too exhausted to move, the Indians went about the task of making a camp. The meat was dressed and a fire built. Soon the odor of wood smoke and cooking drifted through the thickening darkness. The Indians became shadows that slid in and out of the ring of yellow fire light. For the first time Isaac thought about his family on the Red Banks. He knew that by now they would have missed him. The day had been such a wild nightmare that he had not before this moment had time to be homesick, or to evaluate accurately his position. Suddenly he felt very angry, and he hated the Indians bitterly. "If I can grab a gun I will kill them," he thought, but he knew he could not kill them all. "Tonight I will run away," he decided. "When the

Indians are asleep I'll crawl away into the forest and then get up and run until I find the searching party that by now is certainly following our trail."

Then as he felt the ache in his legs and saw the dark tangled mass of forest beyond the firelight, he knew that it was hopeless. He was too tired to go far, even if he could find his directions, which he knew he could never do in the dark cloudy night. He also knew that if he attempted to escape and was recaptured the Indians would surely kill him.

The soft thick layers of leaves beneath his tired body felt deliciously refreshing, but his heart and mind were deeply troubled. He wondered how far they had come. He wondered how many hours had passed before the folks in the village discovered what had happened. He thought of his mother and remembered how she looked that morning . . . now so very long ago it seemed . . . as she bent over the fire to cook breakfast. He could almost smell the clean soap fragrance of her cheek that he had kissed good morning, and he knew now those cheeks were wet with tears for him. He had always hated to see his mother cry.

He looked up into the black sky which had no stars. The light of the fire flickered and faded upon the branches above. He could feel his eyes fill up and overflow in great cool rivulets down his hot cheeks. "Only girls cry," his brother Josh had said. But I guess there is a time when everybody has to cry a little, Isaac decided. He remembered even his father had cried when Grandma Knight died.

His thoughts were swimming far behind the mist of tears when he was pulled back suddenly into reality by someone shaking his shoulder. As he wiped his eyes on the backs of his hands he saw his captor standing over him.

"Eat," said the Indian, thrusting into his hand a stick that pierced a big chunk of sizzling bear meat.

His first impulse was to fling the meat back at the Indian and cry, "I hate you! I hate you! I hate you! You filthy savage, and I won't eat your dirty old grub." But his stomach was aching so with hunger that he didn't say it and began to

24

gnaw the charred meat like a starved dog. It even tasted good.

After his first hunger pains were satisfied he ate more slowly and thought again of home . . . how he had sat with his brothers and sisters around the family table the evening before. The evening before . . . it seemed years ago. Then he thought again of breakfast that very morning . . . how he had rushed through the meal and thrust the last piece of corn pone in his pocket as he hurried to the river bank. The last piece of corn pone . . . it should still be in his pocket, for he hadn't eaten it. All day he had been hungry, but in the excitement he hadn't remembered it. Sure enough, it was still there, but mashed into a doughy wad of crumbs. He picked the crumbs from his pocket and ate them anyway with the last bit of meat, and he thought his mother's baking had never tasted so good.

After the meal was finished several of the Indians took up long stemmed pipes and smoked tobacco. They talked some among themselves, but in the Red Man's tongue which Isaac could not understand. He watched them as they sat in the circle around the fading fire . . . faces the color of rust, high bones in their cheeks, large black eyes, long shiny black hair. The six Potowatamies wore breech cloths, leggings of animal skins that were embroidered with bead designs and vests of coarse cloth, also embroidered with beads and porcupine quills. On their heads were fur caps with feathers standing upright in the back. Hanging from the caps were long leather thongs decorated with beads, feathers, and tufts of hair. The two Kickapoos were dressed similarly, except that instead of the breech cloths and leggings they wore long trousers made of deer skin. Each Indian had a pouch made of an animal's hide which he carried slung from his shoulder. Each had a blanket and his personal weapons. Three now had rifles. The others carried bows and arrows and an assortment of knives, hatchets and tomahawks which they wore suspended from their belts.

As the talk among them continued they apparently began to discuss the adventures of the expedition, for they brought out the trophies they had acquired. Peter Sprinkle's rifle was examined carefully and appraised, as were the cutting knives that had been used in the cane brake. Then, as the boys watched, before their very eyes two of the Indians drew from their pouches human scalps. There was the one with black curly hair that had been Peter Sprinkle's, and also a smaller one with red hair. There was no doubt then about the fate of little Jacob Upp.

After the scalps were passed from man to man for examination, the owners stretched them over small willow hoops to dry. As soon as this was completed a most terrifying thing happened. With a small knife one of the Indians cut from the under sides of the scalps tiny bits of flesh which he thrust upon the points of long sticks. Then a dance began as the bits of flesh were held over the dying fire. Round and round they went, dancing and chanting. All eight of the savages joined in. At the height of the dance the cooked flesh was eaten, not for the sake of hunger, but as a sort of ritual signifying their success as warriors in actually overcoming, or eating up the white enemy. At first they tried to force the three white boys to join them in the dance, but all three were so frightened and wept so bitterly that their captors finally let them fall back upon the ground.

Isaac could watch no more. He buried his face in his arms and cried until he fell asleep.

Chapter 3

It was not yet daylight when an Indian jerked Isaac to his feet from his bed in the leaves. It was a rude way to be awakened, and at first the boy couldn't figure out where he was, for he had slept like the dead from complete exhaustion. His brain, still dull with sleep, was even slow to understand what was going on around him. He felt every muscle and joint in his body ache.

The camp was all astir. Preparations were under way to renew the march. The Indians were in a hurry to get started for they knew that most certainly a band of white men would pick up their trail again as soon as daylight came. The fire which had long since died was not rekindled. Dried leaves and twigs were scattered over the cold ashes so skillfully that it would have taken a keen eye to discover them. There was no breakfast preparation, and Isaac wondered if they were going to start the day with empty stomachs.

While the Indians were quietly bustling about, Isaac edged his way around through the pale pre-dawn light until he found George Sprinkle. "What do you think they'll do to us?" he whispered.

George shook his head and made no answer. George was remembering what had happened to his brother only yesterday, although now it seemed years ago.

"Do you think we could run away?" asked Isaac.

"They'd catch us and then kill us for sure," said George.

"But my father and your father and all the other men from the Red Banks are following our trail right now, I bet you. If we could get back to them before the Indians catch up with us we'd be safe."

"Sure," answered George, "if we could get back. But how do we know how far behind us they are, or if they're even on the right trail? I want to go home as bad as you, but I don't think we could ever make it now. Maybe in a day or two we will—"

At this point in the brief conversation Isaac's captor, muttering something in his own language, grabbed Isaac by the arm and pulled him away.

"Eat," he said in English, thrusting a piece of cold bear meat into Isaac's hand. It was obvious the Indians did not want the white boys to talk to each other.

Cold bear meat is not an appetizing meal, and particularly not at breakfast time. It had been partially roasted the night before, but now the grease was set and the sinews had dried and toughened until Isaac could scarcely bite into it. His first impulse was to throw it away, but then he remembered the hunger of yesterday and he put the meat into his pocket.

When the march began it was just the same as it had been the day before, except for the weather, which had changed much for the worse during the night. Yesterday's warm spring sun was gone. Instead a raw, cold wind bore down from the northwest, and skies were leaden gray. The tender, green spring leaflets looked frail and wilted when the snow began to come down. The party was facing almost directly into the storm, and the huge, wet, wind-driven flakes plopped them in the face. Isaac remembered an old saying that his father often repeated. "Snow meal, snow a great deal. Big drops, soon stops." The saying proved true, for the snow soon stopped, but the wind continued to be wet and raw. Some of the flakes that had been driven against the trunks of the trees clung there and turned to ice. It was miserable weather to be out in, but typical of the territory in April. Always when the dogwood trees began to bloom there was a cold spell. The settlers called it dogwood winter.

All morning long the party kept up a trotting pace. The boys were spaced among the Indians as they had been the day before. Anyone who lagged received a prod from behind. So, with cheeks stung by the wind and feet wet and sore from too long walking, they stumbled on and on through the soggy, snow-sprinkled forest. This was only the second of many such days that were to bring the captive boys almost unbearable hardships and suffering. Sometimes they would travel all day from dawn until night without stopping for food. Hunger and thirst and fatigue were always with them. When the bear meat was all eaten it was a whole day and a night before a deer was killed to replenish the food supply. Creeks and streams, when they came to them, had to be waded or swam. Wet clothing in the cold north wind made them even more uncomfortable. Then too, as the days passed, the Indians seemed to become more severe and impatient. They were getting tired too. The one who had the shoulder wound turned out to be a regular bully.

When the party came to a stream they usually stopped to drink before they crossed. Once, as little John Upp, who was the smallest, knelt to lift his hands full of water to his face, a savage gave him a brutal kick in the back which sent him sprawling face down in the water. Little John got up dripping and frightened and angry. This was only the first of many incidents in which the boys were kicked and tripped and pushed for no other reason than the amusement of their captors.

Once the bully tripped Isaac as they came to the edge of an embankment so that he was sent tumbling head over heels down the steep incline to land in a pile of sharp edged rocks. Some of the savages thought this was hilariously funny, but when Isaac's personal captor helped him back to his feet Isaac saw that this Indian was not amused by what the others had done.

The next afternoon the bullying came to an abrupt and almost disastrous end. Once more they had stopped to drink at a little stream. This one was clear and cool for it ran over a sandy bottom. When Isaac knelt to put his mouth to the water the bully stepped with full weight on the back of his head and crushed his face into the water and sand. Isaac missed the beginning of what happened next for he came up sputtering with grit and mud in his eyes and nose and mouth. His lips had been scratched by the sharp sand until they bled, and he was generally miserable, although really not badly hurt. His captor was furious when he saw what this other Indian had done to him and gave the culprit a blow that sent him sprawling. A terrific fight followed. By the time Isaac could get the sand out of his eyes to see what was happening the two men were clutching at each other and rolling over and over on the ground. Each had drawn a knife, and it seemed there would be a struggle to the death. Over and over they rolled. First one was on top, and then the other. For a moment the bully seemed to be getting an advantage. Then

29

with a tremendous kick Isaac's captor freed himself.

In an instant both were on their feet again. Around and around they danced, the steel of their knife blades flashing, sparring for an opening. Then, as they went into a clinch again and fell down on the ground, the red blood began to flow. For a moment it looked like one of the knives had found a mark, but it was only that the bully's old shoulder wound had reopened. The blood and the pain of the torn wound, however, seemed to have an effect, for he didn't last much longer. After a few more minutes he was pinned to the ground, and in another second he wuold have had a knife in his throat if the other members of the group hadn't intervened. It was a bitter battle, but it served a purpose. From then on the boys were not unduly mistreated.

Isaac felt much easier in his mind now. Although he was still a prisoner he knew now that his captor was also his protector who would fight for him if necessary.

That night as they sat in the ring of red firelight the Indian stared for a long time at the white boy. Then at last he drew closer and, pointing to himself, said, "Me Yellow Jacket—Yellow Jacket. Say name, Yellow Jacket."

Isaac said the name, although the words seemed to sound strange and hard coming from his own throat. He realized that for several days he had hardly spoken a word.

Then the Indian pointed to Isaac and said with the question in his voice, "You?"

"Isaac Knight is my name."

The Indian didn't understand. "Say again," he demanded.

"Isaac Knight."

"Eye? Eye?" Yellow Jacket repeated the word questioningly, pointing to his eye. "Eye? . . . Sack? . . . Night?" He shook his head in bewilderment. "No good name," he grunted in disgust and turned away.

This was really the first conversation they had together.

Chapter 4

Yellow Jacket was not a bad Indian. He took part in the raids and scalpings and captures and was considered very good at it, but that had been his training as a Potowatami warrior, so he couldn't be blamed too much for his savagery. In his heart there was some kindness and understanding for others. If there hadn't been, Isaac probably would never have survived the long hard days ahead. After he had fought to protect Isaac, the relationship between the two was friendlier, and they stayed together more and more, apart from the others. Like his breed, Yellow Jacket was not talkative, but at times he would try to make some conversation. The only trouble was that he didn't know many English words and Isaac didn't know any Indian, so conversation was not easy.

One thing that continued to trouble Yellow Jacket was Isaac's name. He couldn't figure it out at all. The "sack" or "zack" syllable of the first name left him completely confused. He finally put the "eye" and the "night" parts together and came up with "star"—the night's eye. At first he considered calling Isaac "White Star," but when he thought it over more carefully he decided, "White Star squaw name. No good. You boy." And so the problem was temporarily settled with Isaac being called simply "Boy."

The eighth day after the capture brought a return of the good weather. The night before Isaac had slept beside the trunk of a fallen tree with leaves pulled over him for cover. When he dug his way out next morning he looked upon an entirely different world than he had left the night before. During the night the temperature had risen sharply. Now it seemed almost warm again, but the forest was shrouded in

31

such a thick fog that the outlines of trees only a short distance away looked like wisps of shadows.

There were still embers in the fire, and this morning they were rekindled into a nice blaze that set up a small ring of reddish glow on the mist. Beyond the ring of fire red the fog looked very blue, until the sun popped over the horizon and tinged the whole world with pearl pink and lavender. It didn't take the sun long to drive the fog away, and when the mist lifted there was a bright blue sky above. The forest smelled wet and spring-like. Somewhere a cardinal sang out his notes of "Good cheer! Good cheer!"

At first Isaac wondered why the Indians lingered so long around the fire on such a beautiful morning. Usually they were on the march at the first wink of the sun. This morning they seemed to be discussing something of unusual importance. He could see that something different was about to happen. He would have liked to have slipped nearer George Sprinkle so they could have talked together about it, but George was somewhere on the other side of the encampment. Isaac had been getting along so well with Yellow Jacket that he decided not to risk arousing the Indian's anger by doing something which was forbidden, so he sat quietly against a tree and watched and chewed his strip of venison.

After everybody had finished eating, the warriors, who were now sitting in a circle around the dying fire, passed a pipe of tobacco among them. This too was unusual in the morning. Ordinarily they smoked only around the campfire at night. Isaac suddenly realized that the group was planning to split up.

After awhile all the Indians stood up and went through a ceremonious leave taking. Then the two who were Kickapoos turned abruptly and walked away into the forest. The remaining six Potowatamies and the three captive boys covered the fire and resumed their march.

When Isaac got a chance to speak with Yellow Jacket about it he asked him where the two had gone.

"Kickapoo go home now," replied Yellow Jacket. "Kickapoo village by Tippecanoe."

"Where are we going?" asked Isaac.

"We go home too."

"Is it far from here?"

"Long way, Boy. My village in Illinois country. Long way."

Isaac heaved a sigh at the thought of still having a long way to go. He looked down at his shoes which were beginning to break in the seams. He knew too the soles were getting thin for he could feel the rocks under foot pressing through. Also, his coat and trousers were torn and dirty. "A long way to go . . ."

One thing he noticed was that they had altered their course. Every day since his capture they had been walking toward the north, always toward the north. Today they were going almost due west. The sun, as it climbed higher in the cloudless April sky, felt warm on his back.

Although the return of fine weather lifted his spirits for awhile the effect was not lasting. By midday Isaac began to feel peculiar. By mid-afternoon his head was aching so intensely that the jolt of every step made it feel like a little hammer was hitting him between the eyes. He could feel the throb of his pulse in his ears, and his back and legs got so stiff and sore that it was very hard for him to keep going. At first Yellow Jacket was gruff and impatient, but finally he began to realize that his boy was really sick.

As soon as the sun went down Isaac got cold. No matter how close to the fire he lay he shivered until his teeth chattered. That night he ate nothing.

"Warm night. South wind blow," Yellow Jacket kept saying as he sat and watched over the boy. "South wind blow warm. Boy still got winter in bones. Boy sick." Then Yellow Jacket took his own blanket and another which he borrowed from one of the others and wrapped them around Isaac and lay down beside him. "Sleep," he said.

But Isaac couldn't sleep. His chill was so severe that he shivered in spite of the cover and the fire's warmth.

That night was a very long one. He watched the half moon sail high overhead and gild the forest with silver when the fire died. He listened to the forest noises . . . the snapping of a twig, the creaking of a limb against a sudden little breeze, little frogs croaking their first spring songs somewhere away off in a swamp, the cry of a night bird, and close at hand the heavy slow breathing of Yellow Jacket who was fast asleep. Above it all he could hear his own heart beating. There was a great pain in his stomach. As he lay there unsuccessfully trying to go to sleep he began to think of home. He thought of the neat new cabin among the sycamore trees where his brothers were probably at this very moment fast asleep in the loft beneath their clean patchwork quilts. He remembered the rich yellow smell of corn pone just turned out of the pan, and he tried to visualize his brothers around the supper table, recalling an image of each one's face. He thought of his mother and knew that she was probably sleepless too from worry over him. He was again really and truly homesick, and great tears welled up in his eyes so that the moon, when he looked at it, got all blurred and out of shape. He turned on his side with his knees under his chin to try to ease the pain in his legs and back, and at the same time gain a little warmth.

In the almost dead ashes of the fire there were still a few tiny red coals that winked like the tail lights of fire flies on a summer evening. The hours dragged, but finally the moon slipped below the tree tops and the forest grew dark. "It will soon be morning," he thought, "and I will not be able to march. What will they do to me?"

Suddenly he hated the Indians more than ever before, even Yellow Jacket. He felt like he wanted to get up and run away into the forest, and run and run and run until, if nothing better, he dropped down and died. All these thoughts brought a great flood of tears, and he cried bitterly until he fell into a half sleep.

Next day the chills were gone. Instead, he awoke very hot with big beads of perspiration on his forehead, and he discovered that he had kicked off his blankets in his sleep.

Yellow Jacket was pleased. "Boy well now," he said.

But Isaac was far from well. The great throbbing in his head and the pain in his stomach remained. His mouth and tongue were dry and parched, and he was hot all over with a high fever that followed the chills. Nevertheless, the party resumed its march as usual. Isaac thought that he would not survive the day. His feet were heavy like lead as he stumbled along. Every step grew more difficult than the last, until by nightfall he was so very sick that he fell down upon the ground and became delirious. Some of the Indians were frightened and thought that he was possessed by an evil spirit. "Need Medicine Man," they mumbled. One even suggested, "Kill white boy and go away quick." Of course Yellow Jacket would not agree to that. All night he sat by Isaac and held water to his lips when he cried out from thirst.

Next day they did not travel. Some of the Indians threatened to go away anyway, but Yellow Jacket won them over with his argument that rations were so low that they needed a day to send out a hunting party to kill and dress a fresh supply of food for the remainder of the journey. So it was agreed. Two hunters set out toward the north and two to the south. Yellow Jacket watched over Isaac, and the sixth Indian was given the task of guarding George and John so they didn't run away. It was a long day.

When the high fever and delirium finally passed Isaac felt a little better, although he was extremely weak. That night when he propped himself up against a tree to try to eat a bit of the fresh meat the hunters had brought in he noticed that his hands and arms were covered with large red pimples that itched. He could also feel them coming out on his face and body. Suddenly he realized what was wrong with him. His thoughts turned back to the day he had stopped with his family to help the Widow Downs at her cabin along the Green River. Her son, Robert, was in the cabin sick. He remembered it well. That was the day he had probably been exposed, and now he too had smallpox. It was a frightening thing to realize.

"I will die," he thought.

Chapter 5

It was nothing short of a miracle that Isaac did not die. Among the early settlers smallpox was often fatal, even when the patient had the very best care and treatment. Isaac had neither. He was forced to march every day, even when he was so sick he scarcely knew whether he was dead or alive. At night, after a day's travelling, his fever would skyrocket. His sleep, if he got any, was restless. He suffered constantly from thirst, for the Indians carried no water, but depended entirely upon streams for drink when they came to them. Sometimes it would be hours between stops. The smallpox pimples soon covered his entire body and grew into big ugly running sores. No one was ever more miserable. But his strength in some way held out from day to day and finally the worst was over.

One morning about a week after the illness had struck, the party came upon a well-travelled trail in the forest, indicating that they might be approaching an important village or settlement. Walking was easier on the path, and they covered the miles more quickly.

By around noontime, they arrived at an Indian town of some fifty or sixty huts along the banks of a little river the Indians called Mackinaw. As they approached, word of their arrival spread quickly and the whole town turned out to welcome them—men, squaws, children and dogs, all talking and laughing and barking at once. Squaws relieved the travellers of their packs and showed great interest in the white prisoners. Most of their gestures were friendly, but the boys were not exactly appreciative of the attention they got. They didn't like the pats and little pinches they got from the dozens of dirty dark hands that welcomed them.

Isaac could not help noticing, however, that he got far less attention than the other two lads. He realized that he was not very attractive to look at, sick as he was and covered with ugly scabs, but it made him very uncomfortable to see that many of them pointed at him and whispered. Presently Yellow Jacket was swallowed up in the crowd, and Isaac and George and John found themselves surrounded only by the group of jabbering women who led them away to a hut on the other side of the village.

The houses were all very much alike, round with cone shaped thatched roofs. The sides were covered with bark and mats woven of cat-tails and grass tied to a framework of slender poles. Inside a center pole held up the roof, and there was an opening at the very top to let the smoke out when cooking was done indoors on bad days. Around the walls there were pallets of dried grasses and cedar boughs which served as beds. Crude as they were, these were a welcome sight to Isaac. Although he had gradually begun to gain back some of his strength, he was still very weak and walking was tiresome. As soon as he could he dropped down on the nearest bed and stretched his aching limbs.

"Oh how good it feels to rest," he sighed.

"Feeling better today?" asked George.

"Better than I did several days back, I can tell you that." Isaac locked his hands behind his head and stared up into the thatch. "I wonder how many miles we've walked?"

"Seems like a million," piped little John.

"Seems like more than a million to me," said Isaac. "I didn't think I would be alive to see the end of it."

"Neither did I." George sat on the ground and leaned against the center pole with his legs stretched out full length before him. "The question is," he continued, "now that we're here, where are we . . . and how can we get back home?"

"Let's think about that tomorrow," sighed Isaac. "All I want to do now is rest."

"I don't like all these dirty old women pinching me all the time," complained little John. "And this old Indian house

37

stinks." He was not wrong about that. The thatch was permeated with the heavy acrid odor of wood smoke and rancid grease from a whole winter's cooking.

"John, be careful what you say and how you act," warned George. "They seem like they're going to be friendly, so let's don't do anything to make them mad."

"George is right," said Isaac. "If we can make them think we like it here and are satisfied to stay they'll soon quit watching us so closely, and then we'll have a much better chance to get away."

The white boys were, indeed, at the moment a source of great interest in the village. An enthusiastic crowd milled around outside the hut, and the more curious ones peeped in at the door to have a closer look at the pale-skinned strangers.

Presently a young squaw entered carrying a steaming kettle and three bowls with three wooden spoons. She gave the boys a broad white-toothed grin as she set the food on the ground in the midst of them.

"Eat," she said with a giggle, and scurried from the hut.

"Hey, this is not bad," cried George as he sampled the contents of the kettle. "It sure beats raw venison and cold bear meat."

All three boys gathered around the kettle and quickly filled their bowls with a kind of small hominy that had been cooked with a dash of maple sugar. It was such a welcome change from the food they had been forced to eat in the forest that they all had second helpings. Then, when their stomachs were full, it wasn't long until all three were stretched out on the cedar bough beds, fast asleep.

As twilight began to fall the boys awoke and found themselves much refreshed by the food and sleep. The women came again, this time bringing moccasins and Indian garments for John and George. They paid no attention at all to Isaac. John and George were terribly embarrassed when the women began to take away their clothes, but there seemed nothing they could do to prevent it. Soon they were dressed much like the Indian boys they had seen when they came into the village. They couldn't help but grin to see each other looking so ridiculous. Both had loin clothes of skin, held up by belts decorated with beads, and short sleeveless vests embroidered with beads and tiny shells and porcupine quills. They liked their moccasins best for they were soft and comfortable after their own tattered shoes. Then each got a head band of raw hide with feathers stuck in it, and to complete the transformation a squaw brought dyes and painted their faces with red and white and purple stripes. The women giggled and jabbered as the paint was applied. The disguise was so complete that, except for their light skin, the boys would have passed for members of the tribe. When the women were satisfied with the results they led them away.

Isaac was left quite alone in the gathering darkness, wondering why he had been ignored and what was going to happen next. Through the hut door he could see that a huge bonfire was being lighted in the center of the village. Drums and tom-toms began to throb in the night as the flames leapt into the mound of dried branches. He could also see that a great crowd was gathering.

What was going to happen to him? Suddenly he felt uneasy. Why had he not been given Indian clothes like George and John? He remembered how some of the Indians had whispered and pointed at his sores. Was he being left alone just because he was sick, or was there another reason?

The fire suddenly became a frightening thing as he remembered tales he had heard of white people being burned alive by the savages. While he was considering the possibility of slipping outside and running away unnoticed to hide in the forest, some women returned to the hut and motioned him to follow them.

"Come," they said. "Na-mid na-wa-kwa."

Isaac had no idea what "na-mid na-wa-kwa" meant and he was frightened.

"Don't put me in the fire," he cried, but the squaws only grinned broad meaningless grins and repeated, "Come."

Outside hundreds of savages were gathering in a huge ring around the fire. The flames shot high into the air. When the burning twigs crackled and popped, hot red and yellow sparks were spewed out onto the ground. The fire glow turned the hundreds of dark faces to burnished copper. The women who had come for Isaac pulled him by the arms into the midst of the throng and wormed their way through to the front row next to the fire. Here they indicated that he should sit down with a group of women and children who were already there. On the other side of the circle he could see a band of warriors clustered around a large man who wore a many-feathered head dress and carried a tall lance. This, he thought, was probably the chief of the village.

As the music makers increased their tempos the dancing began. First came the tall man leading a sort of snake dance of warriors who pranced behind him in a long wavering line. Around and around the fire they went, shaking rattles and brandishing wands topped with clumps of feathers or animal tails. Isaac noticed the happy expressions on the faces of the dancers and concluded that this was perhaps more of a celebration than a war dance—which, in fact, it was. Among them was Yellow Jacket, stepping very high and looking quite grand in his decorations.

As the dancing got faster and more frantic the audience joined in with chanting and hand clapping until the whole camp was in a commotion. After awhile some women ran into the circle carrying three tall poles. At first Isaac couldn't see what they had fastened at the tops, but when they got around to his side of the fire he recognized the scalps of Peter Sprinkle and John Upp, and a third one. Probably Mr. Downs, he thought, remembering the incident on Green River.

After these women had gone around the fire three times they were joined by several more women who were leading George and John all dressed in their Indian clothes. Had Isaac been certain of his own position he would have surely laughed at his two friends, because they looked very awkward and embarrassed when the squaws prodded them into trying to dance.

40

Isaac kept wondering when his time would come, and what his part in this weird spectacle would be. He sat nervously twisting a piece of leather that had come loose from his shoe sole.

Finally the dancing ended, and then there was wrestling and other contests of strength which the crowd found extremely exciting. Nobody paid the slightest bit of attention to Isaac all evening. He would have found the events much more entertaining if he had known that his role was only that of a spectator. When finally they returned him to the hut two fat old squaws came in and lay down on the beds nearest the door. He did not see John and George any more that night.

For a long time he lay awake thinking and wondering and watching a single star that winked through the opening at the top of the room. The women snored, an owl hooted a long way off in the forest, and at last he too drifted off to sleep.

The day that followed was another day of festivity. During the morning, the entire village went to an open field to watch the young men play lacrosse. There was such a crowd that Isaac thought surely almost all the Indians in the world were gathered there.

It was a bright, beautiful spring day, but cool. Although the players were naked except for their moccasins and their breech clothes the game was so fast and furious that their bronze bodies soon glistened with streams of perspiration as they dashed back and forth across the field after the ball. The playing area took up almost the whole clearing, which Isaac judged was eight hundred to a thousand feet long. Goal posts were set at each end of the field to mark the scoring areas. The number of players on each side seemed to be unlimited and variable, for at times there must have been as many as fifty or sixty on each team. Each player was equipped with a sort of racket or bat made of a stout limb bent at one end into a loop which was laced across with leather thongs so that it resembled, in a crude way, a long handled tennis racket. The playing was rough and tumble. Any tactics seemed permissible. At times it looked like the participants were batting each

41

other more than they were the ball, and once or twice during the day there were even fist fights. Many of the players must have gone home that night with sprains and cuts and bruises, but they all seemed to enjoy themselves thoroughly.

Isaac was interested at first, but after awhile he grew tired of watching the game for he didn't understand the rules. All day long he was chaperoned by the same two old women who had slept in his hut. Sometimes they mumbled to each other, but they made no attempt to talk with him. Even when he tried to speak to them they only shrugged and made no reply. Once he got a glimpse of George and John in the crowd, still dressed in their Indian garments, but he didn't get to speak with them either. He felt very lonely.

At sundown, when the games were over, he was taken back to the hut, still completely bewildered by all that had taken place, and wondering what was to happen in the days to come.

Chapter 6

"Boy . . . Boy!"

Isaac awakened slowly. He turned on his bed and dug his fists into his sleepy eyes. Yellow Jacket was bending over him.

"Boy," he said, "Come. We go home now."

Isaac sat up and stretched his arms and yawned. The round, red sun, just peeping up, cast long slanting shafts of pink light through the hut door. Isaac wasn't fully awake yet, and he hadn't understood what he had heard.

"What did you say?" he asked.

"We go now . . . home," answered Yellow Jacket. "This not my village. We go to my village now. Come."

It hadn't even occurred to Isaac before that Yellow Jacket

did not live here. Perhaps that explained why he had not been treated like the other two boys, why he had not been dressed in Indian clothes and painted as they had been.

"More walking today," he thought with a sigh.

Yellow Jacket drew from his pouch a pair of clean new moccasins. "For Boy," he said, and dropped them on the bed. They were beautiful moccasins of soft deer skin with the hair inside. On the front of each was the figure of a bird worked in colored beads. Isaac couldn't help being pleased.

"Oh, thank you very much," he said. "They're pretty."

There was a broad smile on Yellow Jacket's face. "See?" he said, pointing to the embroidered birds. "Good sign. Put wings on Boy's feet."

The new moccasins were indeed wonderfully comfortable after the hard tattered shoes he had been wearing. He liked the feel of them when he put them on.

It was a magnificent morning. The forest gave off a sweet wet smell. Yellow Jacket said farewell to a few of his friends whom he met as they walked out of the village.

The route they took was toward the west along the river bank. Isaac felt considerably stronger after being well-fed and rested, and Yellow Jacket was in a particularly pleasant and talkative mood. They inspected the villagers' fish traps in the river, and Yellow Jacket pointed out ke-ta-pi-kon, the buffalo fish. Isaac repeated the Indian word after him, "ke-ta-pi-kon." And so it began to be a game to learn the names of things.

They followed the river only a short distance until it veered off to the south, and then they left its banks and struck out through the forest, continuing still in a westerly direction. During the morning they saw "ni-conza," the squirrel, sunning himself on a high limb of "me-tig-wau-bank," the hickory tree. They saw "wah-hoos," the rabbit, scurry away into the thicket, his white tail bobbing after him. Also "nah-hak," the bear, and "wa-waush-ka-she," the deer. Isaac repeated each of the names as Yellow Jacket told them to him, and he was delighted to hear the music of the words as he said them over and over. He learned that forest was "me-tigwa-ki" and the mighty oak tree was "me-tig-goo-meez." "Ab-dak" was the crow, and "she-sheeb" the wild duck. That was the funniest name of all, "she-sheeb." When they came to a pink-flowering Judas tree they paused to watch a butterfly that hovered above the overripe flowers. Even the gentle flutter of its frail yellow wings sent showers of pink petals drifting to the ground.

"Me-men-gwa," said Yellow Jacket, pointing to the delicate lovely creature. "Me-men-gwa." "Me-men-gwa also name of the daughter of my sister, Mi-he-wi," he added. Isaac wondered what a little Indian girl would look like who bore such a beautiful name as Butterfly.

"You will be my white brother," said Yellow Jacket. "I take you to squaw, Wah-be-me-ma, White Dove, my mother. White Dove very wise. She sister to Turkey Foot, once big chief at Potowatami village five days journey to the rising sun. White Dove will know cure for Boy's sores. White Dove very wise."

"You mentioned your sister. Have you got Indian brothers?" asked Isaac.

"No Indian brother now. Little Indian brother die. Wah-be-me-ma very sad. You will take place of Indian brother, make Wah-be-me-ma, White Dove, happy again."

Isaac had no great joy at the prospect of being adopted by the tribe. His great desire was to find a way to escape and return to his family on the Red Banks, but Yellow Jacket's proposition at least promised that he would have good treatment during the time he had to remain with them.

Yellow Jacket carried food in his pouch, fried cakes of corn meal, and a roasted pheasant. They paused to rest and ate part of the rations when the sun was high overhead at midday. The rest of the food they saved until evening. Then they slept side by side beneath a fallen tree on a bed made of leaves and Yellow Jacket's blanket. Travelling had been much more leisurely and pleasant since they had left the others, and Isaac rested peacefully that night without fear, repeating to himself, as he fell asleep, the Indian words he had learned.

The new day dawned as beautiful as the one before. The forest was all sparkly and fragrant with dew and filled with bird song. Since there was only a half day's journey left, Yellow Jacket yawned and stretched and lay lazily in bed.

"We come home today," he said. "Short journey now. We take it easy."

And take it easy they did. Yellow Jacket was no longer the warrior, the captor. He had dropped that guise when they left the others back at the village. Now they were two friends hiking together through the forest. They talked a great deal and examined the things of nature they saw, and Isaac learned many more new words.

Soon after the sun had passed the top of the sky they came out to the bank of another river . . . a very broad, sluggish stream which Yellow Jacket said was the Illinois. They walked along the bank for awhile and presently came opposite a small island, where they stopped while Yellow Jacket cupped his hands around his mouth and sent up a forest-shattering "Wah-hoo" that echoed and re-echoed across the water and into the dark woods around them. In a few moments there was an answer from the island, and a slender red-skinned figure emerged from the bushes and ran to the river's edge. The shouting that followed back and forth between Yellow Jacket and the person on the island was more than Isaac could understand, but he guessed from the joyous gestures and the happy tone of his voice that Yellow Jacket was home at last.

"He Tom-Tom," said Yellow Jacket to Isaac, pointing to the boy across the river. "Tom-Tom son of my sister. He bring canoe. Real name Tom-men-e-gado," added Yellow Jacket laughing. "Me call him Tom-Tom. You like Tom-Tom. Good boy."

And Tom-Tom did bring a canoe. The young Indian dragged the dugout (for that's what it actually was, a hollowed-out log) from beneath the bushes, and with a firm stroke he was no time at all reaching the shore where they were. He bounded from the boat and ran to embrace Yellow Jacket. When they were introduced he offered his hand to Isaac.

The two boys were about the same height and probably about the same age. Tom-Tom was slender and well built and carried himself with the litheness of a young wild animal. His smooth skin was the color of cinnamon and his clear black eyes flashed joy at seeing his uncle again whom, Isaac could see, he admired very much.

As they rowed back to the island Tom-Tom brought Yellow Jacket up to date on what had happened while he was away.

"All braves gone," he said. "They go in many canoes up river. Take furs to Chicagou for trade."

"How long gone?" asked Yellow Jacket.

"Whole moon now. Return soon."

"How is Wah-be-me-ma, my mother?"

"Wah-be-me-ma good. She say today you come back soon."

"How is your little sister, Me-men-gwa?" asked Yellow Jacket.

"Me-men-gwa good . . . grow tall now like woman," replied Tom-Tom.

And so Yellow Jacket got the news of his village.

The island on which they landed was small, but several times longer than it was wide. The village occupied almost all the space, although it was not nearly so large a village as the one they had come from. Isaac guessed there were not more than thirty huts here, arranged among the trees in rows on either side of a sort of avenue cleared through the woods. They came almost at once to the lodge of Wah-be-me-ma.

"White Dove indeed," thought Isaac, when he first saw the fat, greasy old woman sitting at her door stirring a kettle of broth over a small, smoky fire. More like a fat sow than a dove. Her skin was yellowish, paler than Yellow Jacket's, and her greying hair was braided with strips of bright colored cloth into two long plaits that hung over each shoulder. She did not rise when they approached, but she greeted her son warmly when he bent over her to embrace her.

Then Yellow Jacket presented Isaac. The old woman said not a word. A skinny yellow dog came up to sniff at the kettle.

She smacked him a sharp blow with her spoon, which sent him yipping away into the forest, and without so much as wiping it she put the spoon back into the kettle and continued to stir. She looked Isaac up and down with narrow beedy eyes that were set way back in the fat of her face behind her prominent cheek bones.

"He not very pretty," she finally said.

Isaac blushed. Once again he felt self conscious about the scabs and sores that covered his face.

"Boy been sick," explained Yellow Jacket hurriedly. "Much better now. I bring Boy for you to make you happy. Very good boy. You will like."

"Come," she said, rising. "We go to Black Fox."

The three of them walked the length of the village street past the silent gaze of women sitting before their huts in the afternoon sun. Wah-be-me-ma wore many strings of beads and metal ornaments that jingled as she walked.

At the end of the village street was a larger clearing used for a meeting place. A circle of stone in the center was the place where the fires were built. On one side of the clearing was a long rectangular shed with a thatched roof but no sides. Beside it was a lodge similar to the other dwellings in the village, but somewhat larger. At the door sat the oldest looking man Isaac had ever seen. His dark leathery skin was dried and furrowed until his face looked like an old walnut. His long white hair made his skin look even darker by contrast, but there was something special about the old man that made Isaac know at once that he was standing before the chief of the village. Yellow Jacket paid his respects and went immediately into the tale of how he had captured the white boy on the banks of the far away river to bring him home as a present for his mother, and how Isaac had been sick during the journey but was nearly well now, adding that he was a very good boy and had caused no trouble. "Want to make him white brother someday," concluded Yellow Jacket.

Black Fox stared at Isaac for a long time, saying not a word. Isaac felt his face get red again underneath his scabs.

Then, after what seemed a very long time, the old chief raised his bony, trembling hand and said, "Hau," which means, "It is good."

With that the audience was abruptly brought to an end, and Yellow Jacket set out to explore the village to see what changes had taken place during his absence.

Wab-be-me-ma led Isaac straight to the river bank. What happened there was a most unpleasant experience. In spite of his bravest protests, the old squaw stripped him completely of his clothing until he stood bare and naked on the river bank in broad daylight. Then with the sharp edge of a piece of broken clam shell she proceeded to scrape the scabs from each of his small-pox sores. Some of the spots were extremely tender and bled profusely, but even though Isaac howled and danced up and down with the pain, the old woman held him tight and kept on scraping with bulldog tenacity until every scab was removed. Then she made him jump into the river and bathe. The water was like ice. What made Isaac even more furious and embarrassed was to find that Yellow Jacket and Tom-Tom, who had been hiding in the bushes watching the whole operation, were splitting their sides laughing at him.

Although the treatment was severe, it was repeated every day. Every day the scabs were removed and every day he had to take a bath in the cold river. But it seemed to do him good. In a very short space of time he was completely healed and quite well again, except for the deep pitted scars that he would carry for the rest of his life. Because the scars made his skin uneven and bumpy looking, some of the people began to call him Mo-ko-do-mus, which means toad. Wah-be-me-ma and Yellow Jacket didn't approve of the name, and so they vowed he would have a better one on the day of his adoption ceremony.

Chapter 7

April turned into May. Isaac, who now wore Indian garments, became deeply tanned as the warm sun lay on his bare body. Although neither he nor Wah-be-me-ma had been much impressed by one another at their first meeting, they soon became good friends. The old woman was kind. She fed him well and took great delight in preparing his Indian clothes, which she embroidered with intricate bead and quill designs. His thick brown hair had grown quite long since he left home. One day she cut it all off close to his head except a round patch at the crown which was left long, gathered into a sort of tuft and fastened with a silver ornament. He was given wide copper bands to be worn around his arms just below the shoulders, and she pierced his ear lobes for silver rings. All in all, he began to look very much like one of the Potowatamies, except for his blue eyes.

Although he thought of home frequently and contrived all sorts of plans for escape, the days passed rather pleasantly. The matter of escape would not have been difficult. He noticed that the Indians seemed to accept him as a member of the village and soon ceased to keep close watch over his actions. The problem of finding his way home would be the difficult thing. He was afraid that he might not be able to sustain himself for such a long time in the forest, even if he could be fortunate enough to find the way. In the second place, there was always the possibility that he might encounter other roving bands of Indians who would be more savage than the ones he was with. So finally he decided, for the time being at least, to follow the advice of the old saying and "leave well enough alone."

He and Tom-Tom became friends and the two boys learned

to have great fun romping together. "Race you to the river!"
Tom-Tom would cry, and they would take off like two young
deer through the forest with the yellow dog, Ma-heen-gun
(Wolf), barking joyfully at their heels. They had a favorite
swimming hole at the very end of the island where the sand
was soft and smooth and the water dropped to a chin-deep
depth a few feet from shore. With a great leap and a whoop
they would hit the water feet first, making a tremendous
splash. Last one in was a skunk. Both boys were strong swim-
mers, but Tom-Tom could stay under water longer and go a
little faster than Isaac. Even Ma-heen-gun would join in the
fun. He liked to swim out into the middle of the river and
recover the sticks they threw for him. Other days they went
fishing or rowing in Tom-Tom's dug-out.

Sometimes Yellow Jacket accompanied the boys on their
expeditions, but generally they didn't see much of him. Yellow
Jacket was lonesome and restless because all of his friends, the
young warriors his own age, were away on the fur trading mis-
sion. Days in the village were so quiet and uneventful that he
seemed to find life a bore there. Often he would leave at dawn
and not return until evening. Sometimes he brought home
fresh game, sometimes he returned empty handed. Once or
twice he stayed away all night.

Back home on the Green River Isaac had learned from his
brothers how to make a paw-paw whistle. One day he passed
this knowledge along to Tom-Tom to the Indian boy's great
delight.

"You cut a piece like this out of a straight paw-paw branch,"
he explained, holding up a stick eight inches long and as big
around as a man's finger, which he had just cut from a paw-paw
tree in the thicket. "Then you roll it between your hands
until the bark begins to turn loose from the wood—like this—
but be careful and don't break the bark. Then you can slip
the wood out—see?" Tom-Tom watched intently as Isaac slid
the wooden stick in and out of its sleeve of bark. "Next you
make a mouth piece by sticking a short half-round plug in one
end of the bark, like this. Then cut some holes in the top to

50

let the air out, and then you blow and you got a whistle."
Isaac put the whistle to his lips and blew a shrill note which
he could change by sliding the wooden stick in or out. Tom-
Tom laughed with delight.

"Good . . . Good," he cried. "Very good. Now Tom-Tom
make whistle."

"You can have this one," Isaac said.

"No, I make one," insisted Tom-Tom, and he set about
to fashion one just like Isaac's, which he succeeded in doing
quite well.

The boys had fun with the whistles. They devised a secret
code of short and long blasts which they used to signal one
another when they were separated in the forest. Me-men-gwa,
Tom-Tom's little sister, was so fascinated by the whistles that
she wanted one too. Isaac gave her his and made another, better one for himself. Wah-be-me-ma wasn't exactly pleased with
Me-men-gwa for taking up whistle blowing in the village
street. She thought that whistles were more for boys than for
little girls. She told Me-men-gwa that she would make better
use of her time if she would sit with her hand-work.

Isaac liked Me-men-gwa very much, and he thought the
name, Butterfly, was exactly right for her. She was a beautiful
child with pale yellow skin and big black slanting eyes. By
nature she was soft spoken and shy, and she had a delicate air
about her that was different from most Indian girls Isaac had
seen. She was also a favorite of her grandmother, Wah-be-
me-ma, and the old woman had taught her the art of bead
embroidery. For a girl so young she did exceptionally beautiful work. She made a belt for Isaac which he prized highly.
On it were all manner of designs, each with a separate meaning
she said. The two little men among the trees were to represent Isaac and Yellow Jacket, for they had come through the
forest. There were fish and birds and bows and arrows in the
design to represent the hunting and fishing trips that Isaac
and Tom-Tom enjoyed together. There were also the figures
of a boy and a dog which were Tom-Tom and Ma-heen-gun,
and to finish the work, as a sort of signature, a yellow butter-

fly. Isaac thought it was a beautiful belt, and he wore it every day. "This is one thing I will take home with me when I run away from here," he thought.

After the first few sunny days of May the weather turned wet. One morning the sunrise was blood red, and by nightfall late spring rains set in that lasted for three days. When it was too bad to stay outside Isaac and Tom-Tom and Me-men-gwa whiled away the hours playing games together in Wa-be-me-ma's hut, games like jackstraws and guessing games with the walnut shells and the bean. Or they would beg Wah-be-me-ma to tell them stories.

One of the days when it was raining very hard she told them how the Potowatamies became a tribe.

Long ago, according to her version of the story, the Poto-watamies were a part of a great tribe that owned the whole forest extending many days journey in all directions from the big sea waters. The mighty chief was a very cruel man and many of his red brothers did not love him. One day a band of the strongest warriors decided they could not stand it any longer, but would break away from his domain and form a new nation of their own. They built a huge council fire and declared that from that day forward they would rule themselves. Because of this they were given the name Potowatami, because "Potowa" means fire builders and "mi" stands for nation, or the nation which built its own council fire. Isaac thought it was a very wise thing they had done. It reminded him of a story his father had told him about the American colonies and England.

Outside the rain continued to fall without ceasing, great quantities of water that seemed to drop straight down from heaven without effort or vengeance or violence. It made a purring noise on the thatch overhead and ran off in arching silver ribbons into a ditch around the hut that was already overflowing.

Wah-be-me-ma sat combing out her long braids and re-plaiting them with fresh strips of bright cloth.

"Tell us another story," begged Me-men-gwa.

"Yes, the one about when the Great Spirit made the world," urged Tom-Tom.

"Oh yes," cried Me-mem-gwa, "I like that one. It tells about the beautiful maiden and her suitors. Tell us, Wah-be-me-ma."

The old woman continued combing as she began.

"When the Great Spirit, Kitchemonedo, made the world he fill it with creatures that look like men, but who were wicked, ungrateful dogs that never raised their eyes from the ground to thank him for anything. When the Great Spirit see this he is angry and plunged them and the whole world into a great sea of water and drowned them. Then he pick the world up from the water and make a new creature to put upon it. This was a handsome young warrior, and very good. But he was lonely for he was all by himself. Kitchemonedo saw this and took much pity upon him and sent him a sister to cheer him in his loneliness.

"One night the young man had a dream which he tell his sister. In the dream he see five young men come at night to the door of his sister's lodge. 'When these young men come,' he say to her, 'the Great Spirit forbids you to answer, or even smile and look up at the first four. But when the fifth comes, you speak and laugh and show that you are well pleased.' "

Tom-Tom and Me-men-gwa sat almost breathless to hear what would happen next, although probably they had heard the story a hundred times. Ma-heen-gun slunk in unnoticed to get in out of the rain and curled himself up into a wet fur ball at the foot of Isaac's couch. Wah-be-me-ma continued:

"So that night, as the dream foretold, the young men came. The first of the five strangers was Usama. As the young girl had been told she did not look up or smile. The stranger, Usama, fell down and died. The second, whose name was Wa-poko, tried his luck with the fair maiden, but she did not look up or smile, and he too fell down and died. And when the third, Eshkossimin, came, he suffered the same fate. And it was the same with the fourth, No Kees.

"But finally when the fifth, whose name was Montamin,

presented himself, the young maid was laughing and she open the skin-tapestry of her lodge and ask him to come in. Soon the two young lovers are married, and from them the whole race of red-skinned people sprang.

"Then Montamin buried the four unsuccessful suitors, and from their graves plants soon begin to grow. From the grave of Usama come the tobacco. From the grave of Wapoko come the pumpkin. From the grave of Eshkossimin, the melon, and from Ko-kees, the bean.

"And so the Great Spirit provides his new people with something to put in their kettles along with their meat, as well as something they can offer to him as gifts at feasts and ceremonies."

When Wah-be-me-ma finished speaking she rolled a tiny ball of hair she had plucked from her comb and tossed it onto the red coals of the fire. It burned with a flash of flame and a spitting noise.

Isaac thought the story was interesting, but he didn't believe it. He liked the ones about Adam and Eve and Noah and his ark much better, the way his mother used to read them to him from the Holy Book.

Chapter 8

"Boats on the river! Boats on the river!" Pig-tails flying, Me-men-gwa ran as fast as she could, shouting the news.

The village suddenly sprang into a hive of activity. Women and children poured out of every lodge and scurried down to the river bank. When Me-men-gwa couldn't find Tom-Tom and Isaac she guessed they were at their favorite swimming hole, so she didn't stop running until she came to the very end of the island. She wanted to be sure to be the first to tell them the good news, and her guess was right. They were splashing away in the cool water completely unaware that there was any excitement in the village.

"Hurry," she cried, all out of breath. "Boats on the river! Warriors come home!"

Having spread the news now, and not wanting to miss a single bit of the excitement herself, she turned and ran back through the village as fast as she could shouting over her shoulder, "Hurry Tom-Tom, Hurry!"

It didn't take the boys long to scramble into their clothes. Me-heen-gun had been swimming too, and his long yellow hair was soaked. With a vigorous shake that reached from his head to the very tip of his tail he sent a spray of water flying in all directions. Then the three, still dripping, dashed off to join the crowd.

When they arrived at the landing the first canoes were close at hand, and the squaws were waving and shouting to their men. There was great commotion and it was a very happy reunion.

Isaac counted fourteen boats in all, each with two men aboard, and each loaded with all sorts of things that had been acquired by the fur trade. There were blankets and bolts of colored calico, ribbons, silver and copper trinkets, bottles of colored beads, knives of various sizes and shapes, several rifles, gun powder and lead, fish hooks, rope, bags of salt and flour, brass kettles and pans, and many other items, all of which caused great excitement among the women.

According to what Isaac had learned from Tom-Tom, the trading took place at a spot called Chicagou on the shores of the big lake. It was a custom for the men to make the journey there every spring with the furs that had accumulated during the winter hunts. The bargaining was carried on with the white French traders, or sometimes with Indians who acted as agents for the white traders. The returning braves were in a happy mood for they felt they had done extremely well this year.

As the canoes landed they were unloaded, and every woman

and child was given something to carry, so that the whole population looked like a huge pack train as they trudged up the path from the river, through the village and to the rectangular council house at the end of the village street. Here all the new merchandise was piled in assorted stacks to await an equitable distribution which would be worked out later by Chief Black Fox and the leaders of the expedition.

Eagle Feather, the father of Tom-Tom and Me-men-gwa, was among the returning ones, and the children were so happy to see him that Isaac was left quite alone in the excitement. He and the dog, Ma-heen-gun, ended up sitting rather dejectedly at the door of Wah-be-me-ma's hut.

"Where is Yellow Jacket?" the old woman inquired when she returned.

"He left early this morning," said Isaac. "I saw him swim across the river. I guess he hasn't come back yet."

"He be very glad warriors come home. Yellow Jacket not happy last two or three days," she said. "Lonesome I think. He act very strange."

When night came there was a grand celebration. Huge fires were lighted early, and the biggest kettles in the village were put on to cook great quantities of food for the feast that was to be a part of the festivities. While the women were all busy with the preparations, the men bathed themselves in the river, then dressed in their best clothes and feathers and painted their faces.

The sun sank out of the clear sky and in the lemon colored afterlight there was a thin new moon and a big evening star. When darkness fell and the fires began to spread their red glow, the drums started to beat and everybody gathered in the council clearing. Huge cuts of meat roasted on spits over the fires, and some of the women were frying flat corn meal cakes.

Isaac walked to the celebration with Wah-be-me-ma. He always liked to hear the way she jingled.

"Where is Yellow Jacket?" she asked again with worry in her voice. "He should not miss the fun tonight."

It turned out to be a gay evening. There was more than

56

enough food for all, and when everybody had eaten as much as he could hold, the dancing began. First the men who had just returned jumped into the circle around the council fire and did a violent fast step accompanied by the drums and their own shrill whooping. It all made such a din that the whole forest echoed with it. Then the dancers rushed over to the council house where each selected an item from the piles of new merchandise. One took a brass kettle, another a bright shawl, one a white man's patchwork quilt like the one Isaac's mother made, another a length of bright cloth, and so on until each had some article of his choice. As they resumed their dancing they soon drew the women into the circle, and amid a great deal of laughter and merriment each squaw received a gift from her man. Then the warriors dropped out and joined the ring of spectators while the women continued dancing with their new gifts. Even Wah-be-me-ma soon joined them. Her beads and ornaments jingled even more as her fat hulk bounced up and down in time with the music. Around and around the fire they went.

Isaac began to be afraid that soon they would insist that he join in, for already some of the children were in the circle. He was beginning to get a little bored with the whole affair, and he didn't want to be forced into dancing. He would feel silly.

"I don't want to get out there and jump up and down and make a fool of myself," he thought. So while there was still time he managed, on another pretext, to slip out of the crowd and into the darkness beyond the ring of firelight.

The night was dark. The frail young moon had long since gone down, but the stars overhead were wondrously bright and twinkly. He went to the river bank and wandered for awhile along the water's edge. The river was very quiet and the thousands of stars from the sky above reflected in its black surface. The drumming and chanting grew more distant, and he began to feel a great quiet come down around him. Presently he came to the place where the canoes were tied. Tiny little waves were going "plop-plop-plop" against their sides.

He tossed a pebble far out into the darkness and listened for the little splash to echo back. He saw a shooting star and quickly repeated to himself the familiar old rhyme, *Star light, star bright, here's the wish I wish tonight.* And of course, he wished that he would soon find a way to go home.

Suddenly the inspiration came to him as in a flash. "Tonight's the time. I will run away tonight," he thought, "While they're all enjoying the celebration. The men of the village have just come from the place they call Chicagou that lies at the head of this river . . . they've traded with white men there . . . if I can get to white people they will help me . . . I can't possibly lose my way for the river will take me there."

His heart began to pound with excitement. It seemed a good plan and a perfect time. "I won't be missed while the celebration is going on," he told himself. "By the time they find out that one of the boats is missing and suspect that I took it, I'll be so far away that they won't catch me . . . but first I've got to get some food to take along."

The drums were still pounding and the firelight suddenly flared up brighter on the tree tops, indicating that a fresh supply of fuel had been heaped on.

With his pulse throbbing from excitement he ran up the path to the village. Staying as much in the shadows as possible, he stole among the huts until he came to Wah-be-me-ma's where he had been lodged. He knew where the old woman kept smoked fish and meat and grains in huge jars.

"I'll take just enough to keep away starvation," he told himself, "for I don't want to steal from Wah-be-me-ma. And also a blanket to keep myself warm at night. But I must hurry so as to get as far away as possible before they miss me."

The inside of the hut was filled with inky black darkness. He paused at the door and looked in all directions to be sure that no one was nearby to see him. Then he slipped quickly inside and began to feel his way toward the place where the food was stored. He took one step . . . two . . . three . . . and suddenly his foot touched something soft and alive . . . something that moved and uttered a low moan. His breath caught in his throat and his heart skipped a couple of beats. Then a voice in the darkness, very low and shaky, said, "Boy, is that you?"

The voice sounded strange and unnatural, but he recognized the way it called his name. "Yellow Jacket!" he exclaimed. "What's the matter? Why are you lying here?"

The voice was weak. "Yellow Jacket very sick," it said. "Boy, bring water . . . great thirst."

Isaac, still shaking from the fright he had just had, fumbled his way to the door and dipped up a gourd full of water from the jar outside. His hand shook so much that some of the water splashed out on his bare legs. It was cold when it touched his skin and he trembled all the more.

When he knelt in the darkness to find Yellow Jacket's hand that he might give him the gourd of water, he felt the Indian's clothing still wet from the river, which indicated that he had just come home. In contrast his skin felt dry and burning hot from the fever that raged inside him.

"Me got great sickness inside," he moaned. "Great fire in head and stomach. Give me more water."

By now Isaac had completely forgotten why he had come to the hut in the first place. Poor Yellow Jacket. He sounded so very ill. Isaac was frightened. He ran straight over to the celebration and right into the middle of the dancing to fetch Wah-be-me-ma.

Although the poor old woman employed all the knowledge she had of medicines and cures, before the week was over, her son Yellow Jacket was dead from smallpox.

Chapter 9

And so the happy days in the village came to an end. Yellow Jacket's funeral lasted three days. Everybody took part in the mourning and in the various ceremonies and rituals that were held. Although the Indians were generally considered a silent people, it was their custom to show their grief at funerals by wailing and moaning and even shrieking. Not only relatives and close friends, but almost everyone in the village took a turn sitting in the mourners' circle around the body, so the plaintive din was kept up continuously day and night until the time came for the burial. Poor old Wah-be-me-ma was crushed with grief. She became more silent than ever. Instead of wailing and shrieking and making a great noise as the others did, she sat quietly rocking her body back and forth, sobbing silently inside. As a special symbol of her sorrow she cut off her long braids and marked her forehead and cheeks with charcoal. She begged Isaac to stay by her side constantly.

"It is my fault he die," she moaned. "I should had adoption ceremony sooner . . . too late now . . . my fault."

The adoption ceremony she referred to was the one in which Isaac was to have been made her son to take the place of Yellow Jacket's younger brother who had died the winter before. It was the Indians' belief that if a dead person's place was not filled by adoption within a reasonable length of time the departed spirit would return to this world and take away another member of the family. So Wah-be-me-ma blamed Yellow Jacket's death on the fact that she had delayed Isaac's adoption.

"It is my fault he die," she repeated. "My fault!"

Isaac felt very sorry for the poor old woman, and he didn't like to see her blame herself for something that she couldn't help. He even considered explaining to her about smallpox and how Yellow Jacket had become sick because he had been exposed to it. He thought that might somewhat ease her aching conscience, but on the other hand he realized that he would thereby throw the blame onto himself. He knew that now the disease had started in the village there would certainly be other cases breaking out very soon. When that happened it might go hard with him if the people realized that it was he who had brought the sickness to them, so he continued to be sorry for Wah-be-me-ma, but kept silent.

Yellow Jacket's body was washed and oiled and dressed in his finest garments, including an elaborate feather head dress. His face was painted like a warrior, and in his hands they placed a bow and arrow and a tomahawk. At his side were laid a lance, knives, a medicine bag of charms, and other items and trinkets which they thought his spirit would need on its journey to the Happy Hunting Ground. When all that was finished the cedar bough litter upon which he lay was hoisted to the top of four tall poles in the center of the council house, and there it remained until the time of burial.

Isaac watched all the preparations with interest and sadness. Although Yellow Jacket had been his captor, he had learned to become fond of the Indian as a friend. He remembered how Yellow Jacket had fought to protect him from the bully. He remembered how Yellow Jacket had cared for him when he was sick, even though some of the other Indians wanted to kill him. He remembered the pleasant days they had spent together when just the two of them walked in the forest and he learned the red man's names for things. Yellow Jacket had been a good Indian.

All the warriors of the village striped their faces in mourning with black and white paint. During the daytime they followed an old tribal custom and played games that had been the dead man's favorites, lacrosse and the stick relay. The women cooked great kettles of the foods he was known to have been especially fond of. Small portions were placed in little bowls beside the body as offerings to the Great Spirit. The rest was eaten by the people at the funeral feast. During all this time the mourners took turns at keeping up the continuous wailing.

When Isaac was not sitting with Wah-be-me-ma he walked along the river with Tom-Tom, who also had painted his face black and white like the men. They found an old log that the river had washed up, and they would sit on it and swing their bare feet in the water.

"My uncle was good warrior," said Tom-Tom. "Everybody say he be great man some day . . . maybe chief. I am very sad."

"I'm sorry too," said Isaac.

"You like my uncle?" asked Tom-Tom.

"Sure. He was very nice to me, even if he did capture me and take me away from my people. He was a good friend."

"Then you are sorry he die?" asked Tom-Tom.

Isaac knew that his fate would not have been so easy had he been captured by any one of the others. Yellow Jacket had been a good friend, and it was only natural to be sorry to lose him. "Yes . . . yes," he said. "I am very sad . . . like you."

"Then you should paint face like me," said Tom-Tom.

"But I wasn't ever adopted," argued Isaac. "I'm not a member of your tribe."

"No difference. You just the same as brother. You sad. You must paint too," and Tom-Tom took from his skin pouch the dye he had used on his own face and began to rub it onto Isaac's forehead and cheeks. The black was bear grease and soot, and the white was a kind of kaolin clay mixed with oil. It was very sticky and Isaac wasn't at all keen to have the stuff rubbed on his face, but since it was Tom-Tom's wish he didn't resist.

"There now," said Tom-Tom when he finished and leaned back to view his work, "You look more sad."

The yellow dog, Ma-heen-gan, had come with them and was lying on the sand nearby with his head upon his outstretched paws. He opened his big dark eyes and rolled them up to look at the boys when Tom-Tom spoke.

"See, even Ma-heen-gan is very sad," said Tom-Tom. "Come, Ma-heen-gan. I paint your face too."

He pulled the dog up between his knees and rubbed the sooty grease on his muzzle and around his eyes. Ma-heen-gan was used to being played with, so he didn't mind at all. He supposed it was just another game that Tom-Tom had thought up. But when the grease accidentally got into his eyes he shook his head until his ears snapped, and rubbed his face with his paw.

The big, round, red sun pulled another day over the rim of the west, and the three mourners sat by the river in silence while the sky glowed.

Yellow Jacket was buried on the main bank of the river almost opposite the island. When the funeral was all over the village fell back into a quiet routine.

The women began the spring planting the next day, but there was not the joy in it that usually went along with the first breaking of the ground for a new crop. Ordinarily there was dancing and the singing of appropriate planting songs which turned the event into a sort of holiday. This year there was none of that. The people sensed in Yellow Jacket's death a bad omen, and they seemed to feel that something evil was hanging over them.

Each evening before the moon came up Wah-be-me-ma would ask Isaac to row her across the river to visit the new grave. She would take food with her, a bag of charms and magic medicines, and always a pine torch to light the way. While they sat in the dugout the breeze over the river would tear at the flame and blow tails of brown smoke across the water. Isaac would watch the reflections of the fire and smoke slide up and down the waves that his paddle made. It looked like a fiery dragon swimming in the river beside the boat.

"You my son now," said Wah-be-me-ma one evening. "I

speak with Chief Black Fox very soon to make ceremony." There was a long silence and then she said, "I think I have chosen Indian name for you. I think I call you White Cloud." But she said no more and did not explain why she had chosen that name. Isaac did not ask, but he could not help feeling sorry for the poor old woman.

When they came to the place where Yellow Jacket was buried she gave Isaac the torch and directed him to light a small fire on the head of the grave. "The night is dark," she said. "Make fire to light his spirit on the long journey."

Isaac did as he was told and kindled a small blaze of dry twigs which he collected easily from the underbrush close by. As the little yellow tongues of flame lept up, the sticks crackled merrily and a ring of yellow fire light cleared a circle in the darkness. Wah-be-me-ma caressed the ground with her hands, and then took bits of dried venison from her charm bag and dropped them into the fire one by one. They twisted up and burned with a frying sound and sent up wisps of greasy smoke. Then, mumbling some strange ritual, she sprinkled corn meal on the flames, then herbs from her medicine sack, and finally powdered tobacco. After all her prayers and offerings were finished she moved away into the shadows and sat for a long time wailing in the dark. Ma-heen-gan, who had swum after the boat, was affected by the shrill sounds she uttered and, pointing his nose to the sky, set up a mournful howling too.

Isaac sat alone and waited uneasily. To pass the time he dropped little twigs into the fire one at a time and watched them burn into white ashes. "What a strange place to be in," he thought to himself. "Sitting in the middle of an endless forest at night beside an Indian's grave, an Indian squaw, and a dog howling in the darkness close by." He looked at his Indian clothes and the mocassins he was wearing. "Am I really me . . . is this really happening . . . or am I dreaming it?"

The experience was very weird and a little frightening. He remembered the bright sunshine sparkling on the broad Ohio and the clean, sweet-smelling cabin where he used to live. It seemed a million miles away and a hundred years ago.

"Will I ever see those days again?" he asked himself. A big lump came up in his throat and he could feel the tears begin to gather in the corners of his eyes. They spilled over and slid down his nose.

Finally, when the big, yellow moon, round like a pumpkin, rose up over the tops of the trees Wah-be-me-ma ceased her wailing, and they climbed back into the dugout and returned to the village without speaking a word to each other. Wah-be-me-ma's thoughts were full of her dead warrior son, and Isaac's thoughts were full of home.

Chapter 10

Wah-be-me-ma was never able to carry out her plans for Isaac's adoption. Within two weeks she herself fell ill with smallpox, and a few days later was dead. Like a prairie fire driven by a strong wind, the disease caught hold and swept rapidly from hut to hut. Almost every dawn brought reports of new cases. The close friends who had helped Wah-be-me-ma care for Yellow Jacket during his illness were the first victims. One by one they suffered chills and fever and finally the breaking out of the sores. The attacks were fatal to many. The wailing for the dead mingled with the moans of the dying, and the whole village was thrown into a state of panic. Never before had they known anything like it. Never before had there been a need for a regular medicine man, so there was none among them. Black Fox had always been considered very wise in all things, so it was he, as their chief, who had doubled as medicine man whenever the need had arisen. However, this was a situation far more serious than his knowledge of cures was able to handle.

At first he prescribed the sweat treatment which had worked

before in cases of minor ailments. This was a cure widely used among many of the tribes. At the edge of the river he had a tiny hut built of woven mats laced tightly together so that the wind could not blow through. The sick person was laid inside between rows of red hot stones upon which water was poured. When the cool water struck the hot stones it made billows of steam, creating a sort of steam bath which was believed very good for driving demons out of a sick body. When a patient had been sweated in this manner for several hours he was plunged into the cold water of the river to cleanse away the last of the evil. In a case of smallpox, this was exactly the wrong thing to do. The shock of the cold plunge drove the infection inward and caused many to die within a few hours after they had had the treatment.

Black Fox was deeply troubled. As soon as he realized that his knowledge was not enough to save his people he sent one of his strongest runners to ask the loan of a medicine man from a larger Potowatamie village to the east. He knew the journey would take many days, so in the meantime, as a last resort, he summoned a meeting of the Mitawin.

The Mitawin was a very select, secret society whose members included only the strongest and most important men of the community. Because the Mitawin was strictly secret the sides of the council house were covered with mats before the meeting began. Each member who was well enough to attend prepared himself for the important occasion by fasting, bathing, and painting his forehead with bands of yellow and blue—the blue for trouble and the yellow for courage to overcome it. Each member kept a bag filled with all sorts of secret powerful charms and fetishes which he took with him into the council house. These very unusual bags were among their most treasured possessions. Generally they were made of the whole skin of some small animal such as the beaver or the otter. Often the head and feet and tail were left intact and elaborately ornamented with magnificent porcupine quill and bead designs.

The meeting lasted many hours. No one knew what took place inside, but when at last Black Fox came out he ordered great fires built the length of the village street. As the flames lept up into the night sky an angry red glow flooded the clearing. The members of the Mitawin then appeared with their bodies and faces painted all white like ghosts in the night. Four red lightning streaks painted on their cheeks indicated that great power had been invoked from the Thunder God. Three times they danced around each house where a sick person lay. All the while they shook rattles made of deer hoofs and turtle shells and beat upon brass kettles to drive the evil spirits out. Black Fox was too old and feeble to join the dance, so he tottered from lodge to lodge and, with a white pointed arrow, drew magic signs in the dust before each doorway. Of course, all this did not do the least bit of good, and the epidemic continued to strike down the strong as well as the weak.

During these tragic days Isaac worked harder than he had ever worked in his life. After Wah-be-me-ma died he was like an orphan. At first everyone was so concerned with the sick and dying that no one paid any attention to him. He wandered aimlessly about the village with the dog, Ma-heen-gan, trailing at his heels. Then one day he was taken over by a big sullen Indian whose name he didn't even know. From then on his position was little more than that of a slave laborer. The man kept him busy from dawn until far into the night running here and running there, carrying wood from the forest to refuel the fires, digging graves to bury the dead, and doing all sorts of menial work. Although the man never actually struck him, he often threatened him. "Work more fast or I beat you hard with this stick," he would say.

When the Indians began to realize that the disease was contagious, many of the ones who were still well became afraid to go inside the houses where the sick people were, so it was Isaac whom they forced to carry food and water to the stricken. This was in addition to his other work. No one seemed to care if he got sick and died. However, what they did not know was that Isaac had already had smallpox and therefore would never have the disease again. Of course, Isaac himself knew this, and although he was at times almost exhausted with too much work, he had no fear in tending the sick.

Among the patients he cared for were his last remaining friends, Tom-Tom and Me-men-gwa. Both became ill the same day, about two weeks after their grandmother died. Isaac was sorry to see them looking so pale and thin as they lay on their beds of grass and cedar boughs. When their fever ran high they had wild nightmares and cried out in the night. Isaac did everything he could to make them comfortable and well again. Fortunately both seemed to pass safely through the critical stage of the disease, so he felt they would probably get well again, although he knew it would take time.

Up to now it had been the general opinion in the village that the disease came in with the new merchandise the fur traders had brought from up the river. Black Fox ordered many of the things burned on the fires that he kept kindled in the street to drive the evil spirits away. Finally, when some of the first victims who had lived through the ordeal were well enough to be up and around again, one could not help noticing that they had the same kind of deep scars on their faces that Isaac had. It was like a brand which could not be concealed. Therefore, Isaac knew that without a doubt he would sooner or later be linked with the unhappy days. He overheard two of the squaws talking, and for the first time actually began to be afraid that he would be blamed and punished, or even killed because of it.

Many days passed and the runner who had been sent for the medicine man did not return.

Late one afternoon when Isaac was very tired he sat down on the ground at the edge of the clearing to rest before gathering another arm load of wood. It was nearly the end of June and it had been a very hot day. Ma-heen-gan came up and stuck a cold, damp nose in his ear and gave his cheek a big wet lick. Isaac giggled because it tickled, and he grabbed the

68

dog around the neck, rolled him over on his back, and scratched his stomach. "Nice boy," he said, "good old Ma-heen-gan."

The dog replied by thumping his tail happily on the ground. There had been no rain for weeks and the earth was dry and powdery. His tail stirred up a little dust cloud.

The young corn in the clearing had a pale unhealthy color and the leaves were curled and twisted by the sweltering heat. The frail plants had gone untended and the weeds were almost choking them out. Not even the tiniest breeze stirred. The slim shadows of the forest stretched themselves longer and longer across the corn field as the sun settled lower in the west.

Isaac stroked the dog and sighed. He wiped the sweat from his forehead.

"Ma-heen-gan," he said. "I have been a fool to stay here so long. I will run away for sure this time, and nothing will stop me. You want to come along?"

The dog thumped his tail again in the dust.

Isaac realized that running away might not be so easy this time. For one thing, the fires lighted the village all night, and there were always people in the street going back and forth to take care of the sick. It would be hard to put out a boat without being seen. It would even be more difficult not to get caught stealing food that was necessary for the journey. "But I will do it somehow," he vowed.

As he was about to rise, the long shadow of a man fell across his shoulder. He turned with a start, expecting to see that his overseer had slipped up behind to catch him loafing on the job. Instead he found himself face to face with a tall stranger.

"Hau, gayah-da-sey," said the stranger smiling, which was the Red Man's usual manner of friendly greeting, a phrase that meant simply, "Howdy, friend."

Isaac replied with the Indian word, "Do-ges" . . . "truly."

They stared at one another for a long moment. He was a strongly built man approaching middle age with big muscles in his shoulders and arms and neck. His skin was a dark reddish brown and his eyes very black. Instead of a breech cloth like the braves of the village, he wore long deer skin trousers decorated down the sides with fringe.

Finally he said to Isaac in English, "You no Indian. You have blue eyes. You are white boy."

"Yes," replied Isaac. "I am white."

"How come you live here in Indian village, wear Indian clothes? Are you adopted son?"

"No." As he didn't know who the man was Isaac thought it was best to say as little as possible, so he made no explanation of his position.

"You are captive then?" said the stranger.

"Yes."

"Take me to the chief."

"I wouldn't go into the village if I were you," said Isaac. "Many people are very sick there, and already many have died. You might get the sickness too."

"What sickness?" asked the man. "Is it the white man's plague they call smallpox? I see you have the fresh marks of it on your face."

Isaac was startled. This Indian was very smart. They had talked together for only a moment and already he was guessing the truth about how the epidemic had been started. He avoided making a direct answer and said only, "Things are very bad in the village. It is not good for you to go there."

"I do not fear smallpox, if it is that. When you get smallpox you die or you get well. You have two choices, but either way you never get smallpox again." He smiled at having made a little joke and continued, saying, "See marks on my neck. They are the old marks of smallpox. I got well, so I no longer have fear of it. Take me to the chief."

They found Black Fox in the council house surrounded by several of the important warriors of the community. The old man looked tired and even more feeble than ever. Nothing he had done had helped to relieve his people and he was sick at heart.

70

The stranger presented himself to the old chief. "I am called One Bear," he said. "I am a trader from the Ottawa people to the north. I come in friendship."

"You come in bad times," replied Black Fox. "Evil days are upon my people. Many have already gone to the Great Hunting Ground, and many more will die."

"I offer you and your people sympathy," said the stranger. "I know well the suffering caused among the Indians by the white man's disease. But I come to ask food. I have been on a long journey down the Illinois River. All supplies are gone and now I hasten to return to my people in the Ottawa country."

"You are welcome to food," said Black Fox. "We have very little. Since the evil days come the crops go untended and next winter when the snows fall my people will be hungry, but we do not refuse food to one who comes in friendship."

"I do not ask a great amount, and I will give you in exchange this piece of gold." He held out a shiny gold coin.

Black Fox's eyes came alive at the glitter of the pretty piece of bright metal. "It is good," he said.

Then one of the village warriors spoke. "Stranger, you speak of white man's disease. What is the meaning of this?"

"Your people suffer from a sickness called smallpox which the white man has introduced among the Indians. Many of our race have died from it. Whole villages have been wiped out to the east. I myself have suffered the disease, as you can see by the marks I bear."

One of the warriors leaned close to Black Fox and whispered, "It is the white boy, as I have said before. He has brought the curse upon our village." Then he pointed directly at Isaac. "See the marks on his face."

A silence fell in the council house. Isaac felt the blood drain from his cheeks, and he turned cold all over with fright. This was the direct accusation that he had feared for so long. Black Fox stared at him for a long time.

"You have spoken truly," said Black Fox to the warrior.

"White boy will have to die to save our people. Is it not so, stranger?"

One Bear looked from Black Fox to Isaac and then back to Black Fox. Finally he said, "It may take more than the sacrifice of the white boy. Many tribes have found the only way to stop the disease is to move to new ground and burn the old villages behind them. Your houses are now filled with the evil spirits of the disease. The only way you can destroy them is with fire."

"Then the white boy will die in the fire also," said Black Fox. "We must save our people. Is it not so?"

The warriors mumbled their assent.

Isaac's first impulse was to break away and make a run for it, but he knew he would be caught.

He wanted to cry out and fall on his face before Black Fox and beg for mercy. His whole body quivered as in his imagination he saw the wicked flames licking at his feet.

The inside of the council house was breathless and stifling hot. His head seemed to whirl around and around, and the images of the Indians blurred. He clenched his fists tightly and gritted his teeth hard and said to himself, "I must not faint and I must not cry out." The Indians admired courage in the face of danger, and he knew that any show of fear or weakness on his part would make them despise him all the more.

As he was trying to hold himself together he felt a strong hand grip his arm. It was One Bear who held him and spoke to the Chief. "I will take the white boy away with me. There is no need for him to die. Burn your houses and move to new ground, but give the white boy to me."

"No," cried Black Fox. "That way will not destroy the demon he has brought to us. He must die in fire as I have said."

The warriors mumbled their agreement.

"I will give you more gold in exchange for the boy," said One Bear. He reached beneath his belt and brought out a small

72

bag from which he poured a hand full of gold coins into his palm. "See, gold in exchange for the boy."

"Gold is very pretty," said Black Fox, "but we have little need for ornaments now."

"You do not understand," argued One Bear. "I offer you more than ornaments. This is white man's gold that will buy many things. White man will give you many guns, blankets, and other supplies in exchange for these. I speak truly."

Because Black Fox did not understand the value of money he had a look of doubt on his face.

"It is true," cried Isaac, almost in hysteria. "This is real money, gold money!" He guessed that the coins One Bear held would amount to $500, or even more.

"The sickness has brought you hard times," continued One Bear in a quiet persuasive tone. "You will have no crops, no food when the snows fall. Gold will buy much that you will need. It is very good. I give you my word. Take it."

Black Fox hesitated. Isaac's heart pounded. There was a long silence. Then the old chief drew his warriors to one corner of the room and they talked together for a long time in low tones. Finally he turned back into the room and faced One Bear. "We think you speak wise," he said. "We take gold, you take boy. And now we smoke a pipe."

Chapter 11

Next morning before dawn Isaac and his new master left the village with a small supply of food and started up the Illinois River in a canoe. It was a wonderful morning. The river shimmered with pink and mauve from the reflection of the eastern sky. Trees along the shore were wet with dew and gave off a cool, green damp odor. There was a thin mist on the breast of the river. As the light increased the birds began to sing, and soon Isaac could see them darting in and out among the branches and wheeling and dipping over the stream.

One Bear worked the paddle with a strong skilled stroke and the canoe cut the surface of the water smoothly and effortlessly. Isaac gave a sigh of relief as they passed beyond sight of the village. But life there had not been all bad. There were pleasant times when Yellow Jacket and Wah-be-me-ma lived. He had enjoyed friendships with Tom-Tom and Me-men-gwa and Ma-heen-gan, the dog. As he looked down at the belt he wore, the one Me-men-gwa had made for him, he saw in the bead work the little figures representing all his friends. He hoped that Tom-Tom and Me-men-gwa would soon be well. Although he hated leaving them behind, his life the last few weeks had been so miserable that he was truly glad it was all over. And last night, the terrifying edict that he should die in the fire . . . he shuddered to think of it.

"I thank you for saving my life last night," he said to One Bear.

"It is no good that you should die just because they got smallpox. They took you to the village. It was not your fault. If they had killed you it would not make them better. They are very stupid."

Isaac, of course, did not know it yet, but One Bear was really an agent for white traders at Mackinac. As such, it was his job to arrange with the various tribes to trade their furs for goods and trinkets. Because he had frequent business with white people, he had learned a great deal from them and had acquired a certain degree of civilization that had helped him to cast off some of his old Indian superstitions. Therefore he had good reason to call the primitive Black Fox stupid.

"You gave them a great deal of money for me," said Isaac. "How much was it?"

"I do not know by your reckoning," One Bear replied. "I have not yet learned the white man's way with gold, but it was really nothing. I get more soon. You will make my squaw very happy. She has never had a son, not even a daughter. She and me, we have no children at all, so now you will be a son for us."

The days that followed were pleasant enough. One Bear talked freely and told Isaac many legends of the Ottawa people. He described his journeys among the tribes and told how the trading was conducted. Also he spoke of the ever-growing unrest among the Indians.

"There will be war again," he said. "White man is forever pushing the red man out of his lands. Already the white general is asking for another treaty with the chiefs, but it will be useless. The Ohio River must remain the boundary. It was agreed last year that the Ohio River should be the boundary between us. All the Indian nations want now is the peaceable possession of the small part of their land that is left. We can retreat no further, because the country behind will not supply enough food for our people." One Bear's eyes flashed with indignation as he talked. "The tribes will be forced to fight if the United States try to push us any further. It is said that the great white General Wayne already has many soldiers at Fort Washington preparing for an attack. There will be much bloodshed. You will see."

Isaac listened with keen interest, although he didn't understand all about the treaties and agreements. "Where will the war be?" he asked.

"That is hard to say."

"Will you fight too?"

One Bear shrugged. "I am a trader, not a fighter, but if war comes, who knows?"

They also talked of pleasanter things. He told Isaac about Cherry Blossom, who was to be his adopted mother. He said she was waiting at an encampment near the place called Chicagou.

"I've heard of that place," said Isaac. "What's it like?"

"It is nothing really," said One Bear. "Only a place near the big lake where the people from all the villages in the forest meet to trade their furs. From the end of this river we

75

are now travelling there is only a short walk overland to the Chicagou River, which takes you down to the big lake. A black man named Jean Baptiste has a house there and a trading post, and there are also some Indian houses. That is all. You will see when we pass that way."

"Why do they call it Chicagou?" asked Isaac.

One Bear laughed. "I do not know. Chicagou is a word for a place that smells bad. Some say that once there were many skunks there. Others say it is because there were once many wild onions growing there. I do not know. It is a very funny name."

And so they spent the hours in pleasant conversation. Each day of the journey brought them nearer the river's source and the stream grew narrower. The hot summer sun beat down mercilessly from above and reflected back from the water until Isaac's bare skin was burned to a nut brown. At night they would pull the canoe to the shore and sleep beneath the stars on the cool damp earth near the water's edge.

Finally they arrived at their destination. Isaac knew it was the place as soon as he saw how the river bank was cleared of undergrowth and how the ground around was so well trodden. As they landed, several Indians came down from huts nearby to greet One Bear.

He talked with his friends for awhile and made arrangements to leave the canoe in their care. Then the two travellers set out again, on foot this time, along the wide well-beaten road through the forest. This was the famous portage between the two rivers that One Bear had mentioned before. For many generations the Indians from the Great Lakes country had travelled this way to meet their related tribes in the plains and forests below. The early white explorers and missionaries had also carried their boats over this route from the lake to reach the Illinois River which took them down to the mighty Mississippi. When at last, near the end of that day, they completed the crossing and came to the banks of the Chicagou River, Isaac saw a cluster of frail-looking Indian huts. He could see in a moment, from the way they were built, that this was only a temporary encampment. As they came nearer, a pack of dogs set up a boisterous yapping that brought the curious women to their doors. Suddenly one of them, which he guessed immediately was Cherry Blossom, dashed from her hut and came running down the path to meet them. She welcomed One Bear gleefully.

"I bring you a son," he said to her.

"Ah!" she cried, throwing her arms about Isaac. "A little brown squirrel all my own. It is good."

Cherry Blossom was a tall angular woman with deep set eyes that made her cheek bones seem all the more prominent. She appeared to be several years younger than One Bear. For an Indian she was extremely demonstrative. In her joy at seeing her husband again and gaining a son all in one day, she chattered like a magpie. Her clothing smelled of wood smoke and dried fish, for she had been preserving food for the coming winter. Isaac would have preferred less attention and affection, but she was a kind person and he knew that she meant well.

Instead of delaying the adoption as Wah-be-me-ma had done, Cherry Blossom set about immediately to make preparations. For the next few days she worked feverishly to get everything ready for the ceremony. First she sewed up a pair of beautiful leather trousers for Isaac with fringe down the sides like the ones One Bear wore. Then she made him new moccasins and a cap with wild turkey feathers standing up in the back. Also, there was a feast to prepare. In this she had the help of several neighbor women. One Bear went out on a hunt and brought home a fat buck as his contribution.

When the important night arrived all the Indians from the encampment gathered at the big fire. The buck had been roasting on a spit all afternoon and was turned to a juicy brown. Its delicious smell hung heavy in the air.

An Indian adoption was a serious thing. To them it signified a rebirth for the person who went through the ceremony.

In preparation Isaac was thoroughly washed and scrubbed

by Cherry Blossom. He was not at all pleased to have her bathe him, but she insisted that was the way it should be done. Then she rubbed sweet oil into his skin and dressed him in his new clothes. She herself had new garments, including a red calico blouse and a bright shawl with long fringe.

When the neighbors were all assembled around the council fire, Isaac and Cherry Blossom and One Bear took the seats of honor. Isaac sat in the middle and his feet were placed upon a stone in token of stability and strength. One Bear made a short speech of introduction and stated his intentions. Then, taking Isaac by the hand, he led him around the fire several times to signify the passing of time and the long journey that had brought him to them. Isaac looked at the circle of faces as he moved around the fire. Every eye was upon him. Every face was intensely serious.

When they completed the prescribed number of circuits they stopped in front of Cherry Blossom. She rose and took Isaac's hand in hers and held it palm up. Then One Bear, with a quick precise movement, cut a small gash in the end of Isaac's index finger with a piece of sharp flint. Isaac flinched at the prick of pain, but it didn't really hurt. The big red drops of blood came out one by one and dripped to the ground. This was to signify the draining away of his old life. After a few drops had fallen Cherry Blossom gently wiped the rest away with a piece of cloth. Then One Bear made a similar cut in his own finger and let his blood drop into Isaac's wound. As he did this he raised his face to the sky and in a loud voice chanted:

> "All ye of the heaven, all ye of the air, all ye of
>   the earth,
> Ye hills, valleys, rivers, lakes, trees and grasses,
> Ye birds and animals and insects,
> I bid you all to hear me.
> Into your midst we bring this new life
> Which we will call Niconza.
> Consent ye, consent ye all, I implore,

78

Make his path smooth
That he may travel beyond the four hills."

By the four hills he meant infancy, youth, manhood, and old age, and the appeal to the powers of the earth and the air was in recognition of man's dependence upon the other things of creation. Isaac's new name, Niconza, meant "squirrel," and he remembered the first words Cherry Blossom had said the day they met. "Ah, a little brown squirrel all my own," she had cried.

And so the ceremony was over. Cherry Blossom had a tear in her eye. She stood with her arm around Isaac as the people in the circle gathered about to offer congratulations. Some even brought gifts—a bright trinket or a charm as their token of good wishes. The best present of all, which was a big surprise to Isaac, was a handsome bow that his new father gave him.

"I will teach you to be a good hunter," One Bear said.

Then followed the feasting. The food was excellent. The venison was done to a turn, and there was wild rice with honey, fish cakes, and beans baked with chunks of meat in an earthen vessel. Everybody ate and ate until he could hold no more. Then the men sat late around the dying fire and smoked. Finally somebody brought out a jug of the white man's firewater and several of them ended the night by getting drunk.

Long before this, however, Isaac, or Niconza as he was called now, had crept away to the hut with a full stomach and heavy eyelids and had fallen fast asleep.

Chapter 12

"Sit closer to the front," cried One Bear.

Isaac moved forward in the canoe very carefully so that he wouldn't upset the heavily loaded craft. The boat was piled high with bales of furs and household goods. Cherry Blossom was already in her seat and the moment had come to shove off.

Two other heavily loaded canoes were also ready to sail. A small group of friends and neighbors were gathered on the river bank to see them leave. Amid cheery cries of goodbye, the three long canoes slid into the deep water and turned into the current of the river.

"I will see you in the spring," cried One Bear to his friends on the shore, and dipped his paddle deep into the water.

The canoes were picked up by the current and moved swiftly away. It was a brilliant summer morning and the sun glazed the river with a sheen of silver. Isaac let his hand fall over the side and trail in the cool soft water. It was exciting to be on the move again, heading for new and unknown adventures.

The plan was that the three boats would go far north to the Straits of Mackinac to trade the furs they carried. On the way Cherry Blossom and Isaac would stop off to spend the rest of the summer at a village where her relatives lived, and there they would wait for One Bear's return in the fall. The journey meant a trip over the great Lake Michigan that Isaac had heard so much about, and he couldn't wait to see it.

"When will we come to the big lake?" he asked.

"Soon," replied One Bear.

"Don't be impatient, little Niconza," said Cherry Blossom. "You will see enough of the big lake before the summer ends."

As the sun climbed higher in the cloudless sky the heat came down and danced in little shimmery waves over the dark silent forest that bordered the river. The bales of furs gave off a stale, musky odor.

"Is the big lake very deep?" asked Isaac after a while.

"It is so very deep in spots," answered Cherry Blossom, "that it is said it has no bottom and it is filled with great fish as big as this canoe."

Isaac could hardly believe that. He had never imagined water so deep or a fish so large.

"I will tell you about Kwa-sin, the great fisherman," said Cherry Blossom. Then, to pass away the time, she related the old, old legend that had been handed down from her people:

"Once there was a fisherman named Kwa-sin. He wanted to prove his skill and strength by catching the great sturgeon that lived in the bottom of the lake. Many had seen the big fish swimming in the clear depths, but none had dared to try to catch him because of his great size.

"Kwa-sin prepared his line and bait and went in his canoe to a spot above where the great sturgeon lay. 'Take my bait,' he cried, 'and let us see which is the stronger.'

"Kwa-sin waited a long time. The sturgeon lay quietly on the bottom looking up at him. Finally the sturgeon said to his friend the pickerel, 'Take the bait and break this silly fellow's line.'

"Kwa-sin felt his line tighten, and as he pulled and pulled against the weight of the pickerel the canoe almost stood on end. When he finally got his catch to the surface of the water and saw it was the pickerel he had caught he cried in great disgust, 'Shame! You are not the fish I want. Go back to the bottom of the lake.'

"Then the sturgeon told the sunfish to take the bait. The sunfish seized the bait and, swimming with all his might, he whirled the canoe around and around in circles.

"When Kwa-sin saw that he had caught the sunfish instead of the sturgeon he cried, 'Shame! You are not the fish I want. Go back to the bottom of the lake.'

"With this the great sturgeon became angry. 'I will teach this fool a lesson,' he cried, and with that he darted up from the depths where he lay and, opening his great jaws, swallowed both the canoe and Kwa-sin.

"Down and down in the black chasm of the fish's stomach plunged Kwa-sin. He was in utter darkness. He could feel the great heart beating, so he took his tomahawk from his belt and struck it again and again with all his might until the heart finally became still. Then the great fish rose slowly to the surface and began to drift landward. After awhile Kwa-sin heard him grate upon the pebbles and he knew then for certain the sturgeon was dead.

"Suddenly a gleam of light appeared over Kwa-sin's head, and he heard a flapping of wings and a screaming of birds. As he looked up he saw the glittering eyes of a hundred sea-gulls gazing down on him from an opening above. 'It is our brother, Kwa-sin, the fisherman,' cried the seagulls.

"'I have killed the sturgeon,' he shouted back at them. 'Make the opening larger and free me from this prison.'

"Then the screaming seagulls with their beaks and claws tore the opening wider and released Kwa-sin. For many days the birds had a feast, and forever after they and Kwa-sin remained friends."

That was the end of Cherry Blossom's story, and there was a long silence. The canoe moved swiftly with One Bear's firm stroke.

"Did you like the story, Niconza?" she asked.

"Yes," replied Isaac. "I was thinking about one like it that my mother used to tell. It was about a man named Jonah who got swallowed up by a big fish too."

The sun was climbing near the top of the sky. Suddenly Isaac cried, "A house!—look, a house!"

The canoe was coming opposite a large clearing. In the center stood a sturdy log house and several smaller, shed-like buildings. There was also a boat landing built on piles at the edge of the water.

"Yes," said One Bear. "This is the place called Chicagou

that I told you about. It is where much trading is done. The house is where the black man named Jean Baptiste lives. There are many people here sometimes, both red men and white men, but not at this season."

This was the first real house Isaac had seen since he left the Red Banks, and it made him feel as if he was once again in touch with the old life he used to know. "So this is the Chicagou I have heard so much about," he thought to himself. "But there are no white people here after all."

Apparently even the black man, Jean Baptiste, was not at home. The house was closed and there was no sign of life. The canoes did not stop. Isaac feasted his eyes upon this bit of civilization as long as he could, for it brought back memories of home. He turned to follow the house with his eyes as it slipped away from sight behind them. Even if somebody had been able to predict it, and had told him about it, he would never have been able to imagine the great city of Chicago that would one day arise from that spot.

While he was staring back at the cabin the canoe was approaching the mouth of the river. When at last he turned around to face the front agan his eyes caught the tremendous scene that was opening before them.

"Look! Look!" he cried. "Oh Cherry Blossom, look!" He was suddenly so excited by what he saw that he almost committed the unpardonable sin of standing up in the canoe, which would have most certainly upset the whole lot of them.

"It is as I told you," said Cherry Blossom. "The Lake Michigan is very big."

"But . . . oh . . . look . . . oh!" cried Isaac. "I didn't think it would be like this! I've never seen anything so big."

The canoe was then just leaving the river's mouth and entering the lake. Before them was the breathtaking picture of the beautiful blue water, sun-glazed and wave-dimpled, stretching away as far as the eye could see until it met the sky. Isaac was so excited that he could scarcely control himself —and perhaps a little frightened too.

"Oh look!" he cried again. "There is no land on the other

side! The sky touches the water! Is that the edge of the world?"

One Bear chuckled. It must have been, indeed, a shocking surprise for a boy who had lived all of his life in the close confines of the forest, where the trees crowded close around and spread their sheltering arms overhead, to come out suddenly into a vast openness. He was like a chick who bursts from its shell to see the big wide empty world for the first time.

In the days that followed, the lake was a never-ending source of wonderment for Isaac. The three canoes kept close together and moved parallel to the shore. Always on their right hand there was an ever-changing picture. Sometimes there were great hills of yellow sand blown by the wind. Other times the shore line was rocky and the black-green pines crowded almost down to the water's edge. In other places there were broad flat beaches where the little froth-tipped waves chased one another up the sand.

When the boats pulled in to make camp at evening time Isaac liked to see how many different kinds of shells he could find. He would walk barefoot at the edge of the water until the light faded and the stars came out. At night, before he went to sleep, he would lie and listen to the waves whisper to the sand and the winds murmur in the pines. The forest and the lake were full of secrets. In the morning the sun rose up from behind the trees as he had always seen it do, but in the evening it sank right into the water. Just before the big fiery disc dropped from sight it seemed to float for a moment and cast a long red streak across the lake. Then Cherry Blossom would say, "The day is like a big red goose. The Great Hunter has shot an arrow into her, and soon she will die. See how she bleeds upon the water?"

These were the most thrilling days Isaac had known since he had lived with the Indians. They were free from care, and every moment brought a new experience.

On the seventh day they came to a small island situated about a half a mile from the shore. It was a pleasant place with tall, dark pine trees covering the most of it. At one end there was a fine stretch of sand beach, where a group of happy women and children gathered as their boats approached. This was the island where Cherry Blossom's people lived, and it was here that she and Isaac would spend the rest of the summer while One Bear and the two other canoes completed their journey to Mackinac. It was a joyous homecoming for Cherry Blossom, for she had not seen her people for a year. She took great pride in showing off her newly adopted son.

Life on the island turned out to be pleasant for Isaac. There were Indian boys to play with and exciting things to do. He practiced archery with his new bow, and he learned to fish the lake people's way. Sometimes the boys would go to the mainland and hunt in the forest. It was a big thrill the first time he brought down game with his bow and arrow. The prey was only a rabbit, but he was as proud as if it had been the finest buck in the land.

The weeks passed quickly. Wild asters came in bloom and the dry cicada's song filled the afternoon to show that summer was almost done. One day Cherry Blossom said to Isaac, "Niconza, come with me today. We will go to the mainland and hunt for nebezoon."

"Nebezoon," said Isaac. "What is that?"

Cherry Blossom laughed. "Nebezoon, my son, is medicine. It is the time of year to hunt the herbs and roots that will make you well if you get sick this winter."

Hunting nebezoon was a serious matter with the Indians. Cherry Blossom followed the old rituals that had been taught her by her old grandmother. She prepared the basket and wrappings carefully that were to hold the medicines, and she took along a small bag of sacred tobacco. All day long they roamed deep into the forest hunting the plants and the roots. Cherry Blossom explained that for colds and fevers a good remedy was a tea made from boneset and the bark of the prickly ash. Mandrake was a good purge, and blackberry roots were an astringent. She also collected spikenard, sassafrass, golden seal, dock, sheep sorel, male fern and mint. Each time she plucked a plant she would sprinkle a pinch of the sacred tobacco and chant this gentle song.

"You have promised you would heal the earth,
That you are ready with your healing,
With that promise I now pluck you
Take you for your healing virtues."

If there were seeds on the plant she sang a different song.

"Give me of your healing power,
I come not to destroy you.
So I plant your seeds
Back into the hole from which I take you.
Grow again, and more than fourfold.
Accept my thanks for all your benefits."

As she gently placed the seeds back into the soil she sprinkled the sacred tobacco as an offering to the spirit of the plant.

When they returned to the village she spent hours carefully preparing her collection for drying and for its proper storage against the damaging damp of the coming winter.

During these days Isaac learned many other things as well as the collecting and preparing of medicine. He saw how the women tanned buckskin. He watched the flint chippers shape the arrowheads for the village huntsmen. He helped the boys and girls gather the ripe corn and carry in the big, fat, yellow pumpkins from the field. He collected gourds and made them into bowls and ladles for Cherry Blossom.

The days grew shorter and shorter. Crickets sang in the late afternoon. A few leaves began to show the first touches of red and yellow and a blue haze hung over the forest on the main land.

"Soon One Bear will return," said Cherry Blossom.

Chapter 13

One Bear came back on a bright October day. There was chill in the air, but the clear autumn sun still gave off warmth. The heavy, pungent odor of pine wood smoke from the cook fires hung over the village.

Isaac was lying on his back on a big sunny rock at the tip of the island trying to count the wild geese that passed overhead in great wavering wedges. He saw a canoe approaching from the north, but didn't recognize One Bear until he had come quite near. They shouted and waved back and forth to one another, while Isaac slid down from his rock perch and sprinted around the edge of the water to the sand stretch where boats landed.

"Welcome back!" he cried.

One Bear dragged his canoe onto the sand and gave Isaac a squeeze around the shoulders.

"Niconza, you seem to have grown taller while I was away," he said. "How is Cherry Blossom?"

"She's fine. Did you have a good trip?"

"Good enough, I suppose. What is the news here?"

"I've learned to shoot the bow you gave me. I already killed a rabbit with it."

One Bear gave him a smile of approval. They strode into the village together and took Cherry Blossom quite by surprise. She had her hands in batter up to her wrists, for she was patting out corn meal and fish cakes for supper. There was a flutter of meal as she threw her arms in the air to welcome home her husband. They talked together for a few minutes about the little unimportant things that people talk about when they have just been reunited after a long separation, then she turned to Isaac and said, "Niconza, I must make a feast for my husband tonight. Run to the lodge of my sister, Wah-wah-see, and ask the loan of some maple sugar. I will sweeten the pumpkin stew."

They had an extra special meal that night. One Bear complimented Cherry Blossom on her good cooking and said it was the best supper he had eaten since he went north. Later, many of the people of the village came to sit around their fire to listen to the news he brought from Mackinac. What they were most interested in was news of the threatening war.

"There are bad times ahead," reported One Bear. "They say at Mackinac that the great white chief, Wayne, has moved his army farther north into the red man's territory. It is also said that he is building a great fortification at a place just west of the head of the Miami River."

"Why do not the tribes make war now?" said one of the men. "The winter comes soon and then it will be too late. White men are better supplied for winter warfare than our red brothers."

"There is a report that a band of Miamis attacked a supply train just out of Fort Hamilton and captured twenty wagons loaded with corn," said One Bear.

"Corn is good," said another man. "It will feed us when we are hungry, but it will take more than the capture of twenty wagons of corn to drive the white men out of our lands."

"Are not the great chiefs preparing?" asked another.

"They say that Little Turtle of the Miamis and Blue Jacket of the Shawnees have both gathered together many warriors," answered One Bear.

"Then why don't they strike now? Why do they wait until the white chief has built a fortification?" asked the first man in agitation.

"They also say," continued One Bear, "that many warriors from the Potowatamies, the Piankeshaws, the Kickapoos, and other tribes are moving their families to a great encampment near Grand Glaize on the Maumee River. This is so they will be assembled and ready when the time comes. The English at Fort Miami are promising them aid against the American General."

"Bah!" snorted another Indian. "Are not the English white men too? They are not to be trusted."

Isaac sat quietly in the background and listened to all this talk of war, but said not a word. As the fire burned lower he could feel there was frost in the air. The Indians pulled their blankets closer about them. Finally, one by one, they got up and went to their own lodges.

When all the company had gone One Bear and Cherry Blossom and Isaac also prepared for sleep. When they were all snuggled down in the fresh dry grasses beneath the blankets, One Bear said, "Winter is coming early. I think tomorrow we will move to the mainland."

"Oh, no. I don't want to leave the island," pleaded Cherry Blossom. "Why can't we spend the winter here?"

"This will be a very bad winter," warned One Bear. "All the traders have spoken about how thick the hair grows upon the backs of the animals this year. That is a sure sign. This island is a no good place to spend the winter. The north wind will cut you in two, and the damp of the lake is very bad. We go tomorrow."

"But where will we go?" whined Cherry Blossom.

"I know a lodge on the mainland that was used last winter by a trapper. He will not be there this year. It is not too far from here and it is very sturdy, built in the side of a hill that gives good protection from the north and the west. It will need repair, but I think we can make it very warm without too much work."

"There is no village?" asked Cherry Blossom.

"No village."

"But I don't want to live all alone in the forest."

"It will be better than here. You will see."

Although One Bear's argument about the bad weather was sound, Isaac knew there was another reason why he wanted to move. One Bear was never happy to stay in any Indian village very long. His associations with the white traders had given him a new way of thinking and had brought him a certain degree of civilization that was slightly higher than that of the average tribesman. As he had said of Black Fox and the superstitious councilmen in the Potowatami village, "They are stupid." On the other hand, he had not yet reached a degree of culture that would make him completely acceptable as a member of white man's society. And so, he moved as a lone wolf between the two worlds, never quite fitting into either. He liked Isaac for being white and Cherry Blossom for being Indian. They were as buffers for him, and he preferred that they be with him in his private world apart.

"If you don't want to leave tomorrow," he said to Cherry Blossom, "you can stay behind and make your preparations. Niconza and I will go ahead of you and repair the lodge, but we will come back for you in two or three days. Be ready."

That was his final decree, and Cherry Blossom said no more on the subject, although Isaac knew she was not at all happy at the prospect.

Early next morning One Bear and Isaac set out for the mainland. One Bear turned the canoe into a cove and then up a small stream that flowed through the bright autumn forest. The beech trees had leaves like polished golden coins, which they dropped generously onto the slow moving water. Maples were red and yellow, the sumac a flame of scarlet, the hickory a ripe yellow turning to brown, and the sassafrass a variegation of orange, red and bronze. The brilliance of the foliage seemed even more intense in contrast to the shiny, dark green pines and the deep blue of the autumn sky overhead.

"The world puts on a bright blanket before the winter comes," said One Bear.

After they had followed the stream for about five miles they came to a spot where it passed near the foot of a steep low hill. "This is the place," said One Bear. "Let's see if the trapper's hut is still there."

They beached their canoe, and with the big knife he carried in his belt he hacked a way through the vines that tangled across what once had been a path. In a pleasant draw in the southeast side of the hill they found the remains of what had been a sturdy hut. It had not been occupied for a long time except by the animals of the forest who had taken refuge there. Actually it was more of a dugout than a hut, for a good part of the room was dug into the steep side of the hill. The front wall was constructed of several logs piled on top of one another with earth and stones. The roof had been made of poles covered with pieces of thick sod, but the poles had rotted and the rains of several seasons had washed a lot of the sod away. What portions of the roof remained were covered with tall grass and weeds and blackberry briars. One Bear surveyed the situation and decided the project was not hopeless. "Let's tear away all the old roof and build a new one," he said. "The walls can be repaired easily."

Isaac had a wonderful time the next two days. He worked hard, but he enjoyed what he did, for he was helping to build something with his own hands.

After they had torn away the remains of the old roof, they cut new poles and laid them close together. On top of these they put a heavy thatch of long grasses and reeds, and on top of that a layer of thick rooted sod cut from a meadow. Then they reset the stones that had fallen out of the wall and plastered them in place with mud.

"Let's make a chimney so the smoke will go out better," suggested Isaac.

One Bear had planned to put the fire in the middle of the room in the old Indian way, but he agreed that Isaac's idea was a better one, so they set to work to build a chimney of stones and mud at one corner of the hut. Inside, beneath it, they laid a stone fire pit, and when the first fire was kindled they were both delighted to see how the flames leapt into the opening without leaving a trace of smoke or sparks in the room. Then they leveled the earth floor and tramped it smooth. Next they built bunks along the inner wall and filled them with clean dry grass and leaves.

"I think this is a very nice house," said Isaac. "I hope Cherry Blossom will like it."

"Oh, she will like the house well enough when she gets here," said One Bear. "But she won't want to leave the island. She and her sisters, all they do all day is talk, talk, talk, but when the north wind comes she will be glad we are here."

Each night there was heavy frost. When the sun peeped up in the morning it lighted a world that was all silver plated, every twig and every blade of grass. Sometimes there was a thin skin of ice on the shallow water at the edge of the stream. The cold nights brought the leaves tumbling down in torrents until the forest floor was covered with a thick rustly carpet. Soon all the trees would be bare.

When the house was all completed Isaac and One Bear returned to the island. Cherry Blossom was still in a bit of a huff, but she had packed her things as One Bear had told her and was ready to move.

Actually, they had to make several trips before the moving was completed because the canoe just wouldn't hold everything. There were warm blankets and fur robes, the food she had preserved during the summer, the medicines she had collected, and the household vessels and utensils and many other things.

She finally agreed after they were settled that the house was snug, and after all it wasn't so far away from the island that she couldn't go back for a visit maybe once in awhile.

Isaac spent the remaining few pleasant days of autumn gathering great stores of nuts in the forest and stacking wood in one corner of the room so that there would always be dry fuel when the wet weather came.

As One Bear had predicted, the winter came early and it was severe. The wind cut like a knife and it wasn't many days until the first snow fell. By now Isaac wore long leggings and a heavy coat and hood with the fur on the inside. Cherry Blossom had made them for him. Sometimes he would go hunting with One Bear who taught him the proper way to hold his bow and sight his arrow. He taught him how to make traps for some of the smaller animals. He taught him the various tricks the Indians used to fool the larger game they were stalking. Isaac also learned to dress the meat that he killed. He got a big thrill one evening at being able to surprise Cherry Blossom with a fat wild turkey gobbler he had shot himself.

"I will save his tail feathers and make you a cap for next summer," she promised.

When there was enough food in the house and the weather was bad they all stayed inside. To pass the time they sometimes played games. One of their favorites was played with a gourd and six peach stones. Each of the seeds was painted black on one side. They were placed in the gourd, shaken thoroughly, and then spilled out upon the ground. If all turned up the same color it was worth ten beans to the lucky player. Five of the same color were worth five beans, and four of the same, two beans. If the peach seeds turned up three of each color the player didn't get anything. The gourd was passed from one to another, and when the game was over the one who had been able to collect the most beans was declared the winner. They passed many hours at this.

Sometimes One Bear would go on extended hunting trips alone and stay away for several days at a time. There was one time that Isaac never forgot.

The day One Bear left there was only a few inches of old snow on the ground, but next morning when Isaac and Cherry Blossom awoke a black storm cloud was coming in from the northwest and before the day was very old they were struck by a raging blizzard. Cherry Blossom was frantic with worry.

"I told him not to go because the weather would change," she said. "But he will never listen to a woman."

"Don't worry," said Isaac. "He knows the ways of the forest and he can take care of himself."

"But this is a very bad storm," she said.

All day long the wind howled and whipped the snow before it until there was a drift nearly as high as the roof in front of the door. Finally when night came the sky cleared in the west and the wind ceased, but an intense cold settled down with the darkness. The silence was enormous. The forest was so muffled in snow that not even a limb creaked. Isaac looked up through a crack above the robe that covered the door. The whole world was blue-white in the moonlight. Suddenly a pine bough snapped under the weight of its white load and the noise echoed like a gun shot in the great silence. Then, somewhere away in the distance, a hungry wolf howled.

Two nights later they got the fright of their lives. It was still bitterly cold and they went to bed early to keep warm. Cozy and snug beneath the blankets and fur robes they were soon asleep. Sometime towards the middle of the night they were both startled out of their deep slumber by a snarling noise outside the door.

"Cherry Blossom," whispered Isaac. "Did you hear a noise?"

"Yes," she replied. "The wolves have come down to our door. They are hungry and they smell our meat."

Isaac's blood ran cold. He remembered tales of hungry wolves attacking whole settlements and carrying away animals and even small children. They were alone, just two in an almost endless forest.

Suddenly there was an ear-splitting howl just over their heads and a crunching of snow on the roof. One of the beasts was standing on top of the house just above them. Both Isaac and Cherry Blossom sprang from their beds and felt for one another in the darkness. There was a sniffing at the door, a whine, and then a snarl and a snap as one wolf struck at another who had come too near. Suddenly Isaac felt a new surge of courage. With One Bear away he was the man of the house.

"Don't be afraid, Cherry Blossom," he said, although his voice was shaking. "If they tear down the door I'll kill them with my bow and arrow."

"No . . . no, Niconza," said Cherry Blossom. "You are very

94

brave, but the best you could do would be to kill only one. There are many in the pack, and they would be upon us faster than you could use your bow."

Isaac knew she spoke the truth. "But what are we going to do?" he asked in a whisper.

"I have an idea," replied Cherry Blossom. "They are hungry. I will feed them."

"Oh no," cried Isaac. "Don't do that. That would make them all the hungrier so they'd want to eat us too."

"I do not think so," she said, and she reached beneath her blankets and pulled a handful of dry grass from her bed. "Here," she said, handing the grass to Isaac. "Go blow upon the coals and twist this into a torch. Light it and stand behind the door. Wolves do not like fire, and they won't try to come in while the flame is burning. Now I will fix their feast."

Isaac did as he was told, and he could tell from the sounds outside that the animals withdrew when he came near the door with the fire. The flame crackled in the dry grass and sent up clouds of grey smoke which soon filled the room. Bits of the grass burned free and dropped flaming to his feet.

Meanwhile Cherry Blossom was busy. She took two chunks of fresh raw venison she had stored away from One Bear's latest kill. Then from her pouch of medicines and charms she took a small bag that contained tiny sharp chips of flint which she had collected from the arrow-head maker's. Quickly she worked many of these sharp bits of stone into the folds of the meat.

"Make a bigger and brighter torch, Niconza," she said. "I am ready to feed the wolves."

"I'm afraid," Isaac acknowledged. "I don't think you should give them food."

"Quick! Do as I tell you," she snapped.

Isaac made another bigger torch and lighted it.

"Now," said Cherry Blossom. "Pull back the robe from the door and hold the torch high."

95

Isaac was trembling with fright. He hesitated a moment and then pulled the robe from the doorway. The flame made a yellow glow on the snow. Beyond the ring of firelight he could see a circle of red eyes gleaming out of the cold darkness.

Cherry Blossom stepped outside the door with the meat in her hands. Her breath was white on the frozen air. Isaac could hear his heart beating thump, thump, thump in his ears. With all her might she hurled the meat as far as she could into the pack of hungry animals—first one piece, and then the other. They landed with a soft plop in the snow.

"Quick!" she cried. "Put out the torch and come inside."

Almost at once there was a horrible commotion. What happened was that the hungry beasts pounced upon the food and began to tear it apart with their fangs, but the sharp bits of flint that Cherry Blossom had put into it cut their tongues and mouths. Maddened by the stabbing pain of the flint cuts and the smell and taste of the fresh warm blood that flowed from their wounds, they began to attack one another. A most horrible fight followed. Isaac had seen and heard dog fights before, but never anything like this. It went on for the better part of an hour . . . the snarling, snapping, howling, crying out . . . a noise that fairly split the silence of the snow-filled forest. Finally, completely exhausted, torn, bleeding, some perhaps dying, the wolves dragged themselves away through the snow, and silence settled down once again.

"I think that will take care of them for tonight," said Cherry Blossom. "Let us sleep now."

Of course Isaac didn't sleep anymore that night. When daylight came he went outside to see what had happened. The snow had been stained with blood and mixed with tufts of hair. It was churned and turned up, thawed by the heat of the animals' bodies, and trampled and refrozen. Where yesterday they had been only smooth unbroken whiteness, now there was a great, ugly, dirty, red-stained scar to mark where the battle had taken place.

Late that afternoon One Bear returned. Isaac couldn't wait

to tell him of their experience, and how they had driven the beasts away.

"I saw bloody tracks far out in the forest," he said. "I wondered who had been hunting wolves."

"Or who the wolves had been hunting?" snapped Cherry Blossom.

Chapter 14

Winter dragged by slowly. One Bear trapped and hunted and collected a valuable store of fine furs. Cherry Blossom was lonesome and irritable because she longed for the spring to come so she could return to the village. Sometimes she was quarrelsome with One Bear, but most of the time he didn't let it bother him. Because she was much younger than he, and because he was really fond of her, it seemed that he treated her more like a peevish child than a wife. He allowed her much more freedom of tongue than most squaws enjoyed, sometimes even giving in to her whims. But he was tolerant only up to a point, and she knew exactly when that point was reached. When he made a final decree the case in question was closed, and she knew well enough to drop the matter.

Gradually the days grew longer and the sun's warmth increased. The snow finally melted away and the first sprigs of green appeared in the sunny sheltered spots. Then she ventured forth to hunt for the tender young shoots of dock and lamb's quarter and poke, which she cooked in a big kettle for supper, and life became pleasanter. "Greens are good for the blood in the spring," she said.

When the sap began to rise in the maple trees the Indian villages came to life. Groups of women and children came from the island to set up a sugar camp on the mainland, and

Cherry Blossom and Isaac went out to join them. One Bear and a group of other men set out in their canoes for Jean Baptiste's trading post at Chicagou. Then spring had finally come.

Sugar making was like a festival for the women and children. They worked hard all day, but at night they danced and played games around the camp fire. Isaac helped the boys and girls collect the sap. Small holes were cut in the bark of the maple trees, and hollow reeds were stuck into the holes to serve as spouts for draining away the precious fluid. Big hollow gourds were hung beneath the spouts to catch the sap as it dripped out. It was the children's job to make regular rounds of the tapped trees and watch the gourds to see that they didn't get too full and run over. The women poured the sap they collected into big kettles and boiled it over slow fires until it became thick and crystalline. They all had tasting sticks which they would dip into the kettles from time to time to sample the sweet sticky syrup. It was delicious. Everybody had a good time.

When the sugar making was over Cherry Blossom and Isaac went back to live on the island with the others until One Bear returned. Cherry Blossom was glad to be with her people again. She kept busy every day with spring chores. She made Isaac new trousers and moccasins of soft deer skin. His thick dark hair had grown almost to his shoulders during the winter, so she gave him a new, short spring hair cut which felt good.

Spring flowers bloomed in the forest, the trees put on their tender new leaves, the birds returned to nest in the thickets, and the blue lake sparkled under the clear warm sun. Isaac and the Indian boys fished, played lacrosse, and even braved the cold water for an occasional quick swim. Life was carefree and pleasant.

One Bear had said that as soon as he returned from Chicagou he would go on to the Straits of Mackinac. Cherry Blossom had a secret desire to make the trip with him, but one thing troubled her. She had grown to love Isaac as her own son, but she knew deep in her heart that since he was a white boy he would go back to his own people if he ever had an opportunity. She knew that if they took him to Mackinac he would probably see white men. She was afraid that he might run away.

There was an old woman in the village who was known to be a witch and a fortune teller. She was a skinny, toothless old crone with dim, watery eyes and scraggly, grey hair. She sat all day in her hut and mixed her magic potions and mumbled strange incantations to herself. The people said she could cast spells and lay curses on her enemies, but she had become a sort of pet in the village and no one could ever remember that she had done evil to any person who lived there. Some said that on nights when the full moon reached the top of the sky she would turn herself into a grey vixen and run through the forest, but no one had ever actually seen her do it. Besides all this she had the power to look into the future.

Cherry Blossom pondered over her problem for many days, but she could not reach a decision. She wanted very much to go to Mackinac, but she didn't want to risk losing her Niconza. Finally one day she decided to go to the old woman of magic. "Old mother," she said. "You are a wise one who has seen many summers. Will you look into the future and tell me what I should do?"

The old woman squinted at her with her weak, old eyes. "You are named Cherry Blossom," she said in her creaky old voice, "You are daughter of South Wind. I remember you when you were papoose."

"That is true," replied Cherry Blossom. "My mother was called South Wind."

"Sit down, daughter," she said, "and give me three hairs from your head."

Cherry Blossom pulled three long, black hairs from her braid and gave them to the old witch. The old woman mumbled something and dropped them into an earthen bowl of oil that sat before her. Then as she chanted a strange little song she sprinkled Cherry Blossom's head with a tiny bundle of witchhazel twigs that had been dipped into the same oil.

Cherry Blossom squirmed. The hut was dark and hot and evil smelling.

"You do not live in village always," the old woman said.

"No, my husband is a trader. I come here when he is on long journeys."

"You have always been a strange one," the old woman continued. "You have never had papoose, though you have been married nine summers."

"No," replied Cherry Blossom. "I have never had a papoose, but I have an adopted son that I call Niconza."

"I know . . . I know," squeaked the old woman impatiently, "I was coming to that."

She moved the bowl of oil between herself and Cherry Blossom and lighted it with a twig from her fire. The oil burned with a thin blue flame and the hairs curled and twisted like snakes. Into this flame she sprinkled some powder from her magic bag. Suddenly a great curtain of blue smoke rose up from the bowl, so thick they could scarcely see one another. The old woman jangled a string of painted shells and mumbled to herself. Then suddenly, in an entirely different voice, a voice much lower than the one she had spoken in before, she said, very slowly, "I see in the smoke you take long journey over the water . . . long journey to the land where the north wind lives."

"Yes," stammered Cherry Blossom, completely surprised. "I was just thinking of such a journey. I hope to go with my husband to the straits of Mackinac when he returns from Chicagou."

"He will return, but not as soon as you hope . . . I see a boy you call your son sitting in canoe between you . . . he is not one of our people."

Cherry Blossom was amazed by the old woman's knowledge. "I am hoping to take him on this journey with us. But tell me, old mother, is it safe to take my son there? Maybe I should leave him here at the village with my sister."

The old woman stirred a circle in the smoke with her hands and peered deep into it. "It is better you should take your son with you. Do not leave him with your sister. You would be sorry for that."

"I am very glad you tell me this," said Cherry Blossom. "It is what I wanted to know."

"But beware!" shrieked the old woman, pointing her long bony finger through the smoke curtain almost into Cherry Blossoms' face. "BEWARE! See that the boy does not make talk with white men in the north . . . or you will lose him."

Cherry Blossom sat silent for a moment. "That is what I fear. Do you really think it is safe for me to take him with us?"

"It is safe if you take care . . . I have told you only what I see in the smoke."

There was a finality in the last words which told Cherry Blossom that the audience was at an end.

"Thank you, old mother," she said, and she got up and walked out of the dark smoky hut into the bright spring sunshine. She looked fondly at Isaac who was playing a ball game with the boys in the village street.

Chapter 15

One Bear returned from Chicagou in the soft twilight of an early summer evening. He brought more news of the uneasiness among the tribes and the preparations they were making for war against the ever advancing armies of the American General, Anthony Wayne. When they heard this, twelve of the young braves in the village, itching for excitement and adventure, decided to go and join the forces of the great Chief Little Turtle. To prepare themselves for war they fasted for three days, took the sweat treatment to purify themselves, and bathed their bodies in the lake.

The women made a great feast, and on the night before

they left the whole village turned out for a big celebration. The young warriors smeared their faces and bodies with red and black paint and dressed in their finest feathered head gear. All night they danced around the council fire. The deep throated drums throbbed the rhythm, and with all the whooping and the shaking of rattles it was a spirited and noisy farewell party. When the dawn came they sailed away in six canoes which the women and girls had decorated with flowers and sprigs of pine.

A few days after this One Bear made preparations for his trip to the straits of Mackinac. Cherry Blossom told him of her visit to the witch and of the advice the old woman had given her. She asked him to take her and Isaac with him. He said no at first when she nagged, but later, after she changed her tactics from nagging to pleading, he finally agreed.

The long canoe trip up Lake Michigan turned out to be another happy adventure for Isaac. The distance was great and it took many days to complete the journey. The canoe was heavily loaded with furs, just as it had been the year before when they came from Chicagou to the island. On nights when it looked like rain they would unload the furs and pile them on some high, well-drained spot and turn the canoe upside down over them to keep them dry. Sometimes they would pull in to shore at mid-day and Isaac and One Bear would go into the forest to hunt small game for food.

"It is good to stretch the legs," One Bear said.

Cherry Blossom would stay behind on the beach and heat stones to bake corn meal cakes.

On these inshore hunting trips they saw a great many deer, more deer than Isaac had ever seen before. Many times he was certain he could have brought one down with his bow and arrow. Always One Bear said, "No, Niconza. Do not kill the deer. While we travel we cannot use that much meat. It would be a waste. Aim your arrow instead at a rabbit or the squirrel."

After many pleasant days they came to the northernmost end of Lake Michigan and entered the narrow waters called the Straits of Mackinac. Then they came to the lovely island which the Indians in the very early days had called Michili-mackinac. This meant "the great turtle," but One Bear always called it by the short name, Mackinac, which he had learned from the white men. It was a place of pleasant forests and strange rock formations. An old legend said it had been dropped there in the water by the hand of the Great Spirit.

There had been a fort on the island for many years, held first by the French, and then by the English. Because of its important position between Lake Michigan and Lake Huron, it was one of the busiest trading posts on the frontier, and a town had grown up on the waterfront where the tall masted sailing ships came to rest. The Indians who came in the trading seasons lived in a sort of transient camp they had established on the other end of the island.

When One Bear and Cherry Blossom and Isaac got to the camp they found many Indians had arrived before them. The pine woods were filled with all sorts of temporary huts and shelters. The odor of smoke and cooking hung heavily under the thick branches. They spent the first day building a hut for themselves. It was flimsy kind of shelter made of poles and branches with skins and blankets tied down over the top, but they thought it would serve well enough for the short time they planned to stay. It was summertime anyway. Finally settled, the day came to go into the town. Isaac had been eagerly looking forward to this.

The town was a brawling frontier village of some twenty or more log houses facing the water front and protected from the rear by a high rocky bluff topped by the fort. Three tall masted sailing vessels were tied up at the dock, and the sailors scurried up and down the gangplanks loading and unloading barrels and boxes and bales of furs. Isaac was amazed at the size and beauty of these big ships. He had never seen anything like them on the Ohio River.

Indians from many tribes were in town to trade their furs for blankets and supplies. They clustered in groups to bargain with the white merchants and traders.

It was said that every pelt that came from the northwest

103

and every package of goods that went there passed through Mackinac. Isaac had never seen such a large town and so much activity.

While One Bear was busy with his trading, Isaac and Cherry Blossom strolled along the waterfront and through the village. Red coated British soldiers from the garrison loitered in front of the wharfside tavern. At one store Cherry Blossom spied a bolt of red calico that she thought was the prettiest cloth she had ever seen.

"Oh look. Niconza!" she exclaimed. "See the pretty cloth? I would like to make a new dress out of that." She gazed longingly at the material. "I will ask One Bear to get it for me."

"Do you want me to go find him and bring him here?" asked Isaac.

"No, not now. I will ask him for the cloth in my own time."

She couldn't resist moving closer so that she could take the bright material in her hands and feel its smooth texture. When she did this a white woman, who was apparently the wife of the store's owner, came up to talk with her. Isaac thought he had never seen such a beautiful, kind looking woman. Her smooth yellow hair was rolled into a big knot at the back of her head and she wore a clean blue dress and a freshly ironed white apron. When she came close he noticed that she smelled good. Suddenly he remembered his mother and was homesick. He realized that he hadn't thought much of home for a long time. It all seemed so long ago and very far away.

When the woman spoke to Cherry Blossom her voice was soft and musical. "This is very good cloth," she said, "and very new. It has just come from the east by the last boat."

Cherry Blossom held the end of the bolt up to her shoulder and admired the rich red color. "I will ask my husband to come here and get this for me," she said. "He has very good furs this year."

"We will be very glad to bargain with your husband," the white lady said. Then she turned to Isaac and smiled. "Would you like a piece of butter bread with jam?" she asked. Isaac thought it was the most beautiful smile he had ever seen.

Cherry Blossom started to leave as soon as the white woman spoke to Isaac.

"Wait just a minute," the lady said. "Don't go away. Let me give the boy something to eat." When she went into another room Cherry Blossom took Isaac by the arm and said, "Come, Niconza, we will go."

They had just gone into the street when the kind woman came running out the door. "Here little boy," she called. "Don't you want this nice piece of bread? It is fresh out of the oven."

Isaac hesitated. He looked at Cherry Blossom. She was frowning. He pulled away from her grasp and ran back to the woman. As she handed him the bread she whispered, "You are a white boy, aren't you?"

"Yes ma'am," he replied.

"Niconza! Niconza!" cried Cherry Blossom. "Let us go now." She came running back to pull him away by the arm before he could even thank the woman.

The bread was still warm from the oven and the fresh butter and sweet thick berry jam tasted wonderful. It was the first white man's bread he had tasted for almost a year and a half, and just eating it made him think more than ever of his mother's warm fragrant kitchen.

Cherry Blossom didn't want to stay in the town any longer. Her brow was furrowed, and it was plain to see that she was worried. "Let us go back to the camp," she said. "I am tired."

Isaac knew this was only an excuse to get him away from the white people, for Cherry Blossom was never tired. She was strong as an ox.

It was a lazy hot afternoon. The Indian women back at the camp chattered together and Isaac lay at the foot of a pine tree and watched the fuzzy white clouds sail slowly across the blue sky. His thoughts were divided between the beautiful lady in the town who had been kind to him and his mother who was so very far away. Toward evening he heard some excitement at the edge of the camp. When he looked up he saw a group of Indians gathered around a red coated soldier who had just ridden in on a black horse. Cherry Blossom saw him too.

"Niconza," she cried. "Come inside."

Isaac obeyed reluctantly, but he stayed near the door where he could look out to see what was going to happen. Presently the soldier came in their direction, and Isaac could hear him say, "They tell me in the town that you Indians are holding a white boy captive. I want to see him."

Isaac's heart jumped.

"Niconza, stay inside," snapped Cherry Blossom, and she planted herself firmly in the door in front of him.

When the soldier began to make threats, the Indians got more and more excited and a little angry, although many of them were perhaps secretly frightened in the presence of a uniformed soldier. Finally an Indian woman several huts away broke down under his threats and pointed to Cherry Blossom. Cherry Blossom's anger flared. She shouted insults at the woman who had betrayed her and faced the soldier squarely.

"Are you the one who holds a white boy captive?" he asked her bluntly.

"I hold no one captive," she snapped.

"The squaw says you have a white boy in your tent. Let me see him."

"I hold no one captive!" she screamed. "That squaw is a meddlesome old witch. I will poke out her eyes."

The soldier's eyes flashed. "Come on, woman, show me the boy."

"I have no one here but my own son," cried Cherry Blossom.

By this time a great crowd of Indians had gathered around the soldier. Some of them were frightened, but most of them were getting angry and began to throw insulting remarks at him. It looked as if the whole affair might flare into serious trouble.

The soldier moved toward Cherry Blossom as if he intended to push her away from the door. At this the Indians began to crowd around him. One or two of the men let their hands slide to the knives in their belts.

"I have no one here but my own son, Niconza," she cried. "He is my own son that I have adopted by the ritual of my husband's family. He is mine."

Isaac had been watching all of this with mounting interest and excitement. Finally he gathered his courage and stepped out past Cherry Blossom. The soldier stared at him for a minute.

"You are the white boy they told me about in the town. I have come to take you away."

Cherry Blossom threw her arms around Isaac. "No! No!" she screamed. "He is my adopted son. You have no right." They all stood glaring at one another for what seemed a long time.

"Well, come on, boy," snapped the soldier. "What are you waiting for? Don't you want to go back to your own people?"

Isaac was frightened. He looked at the angry faces of the Indians. He looked up at Cherry Blossom whose face was both frightened and furious. He could feel her tremble as she held him tightly. His throat was tight and dry. Finally he heard himself say in a small uncertain voice, "I guess I want to stay here."

He didn't know why he had said it, except he knew in his heart that if he had tried to go away with the soldier it would have made trouble between the Indians and the white people in the village, maybe even a war.

"All right," snapped the soldier. "If you want to stay with these savages I guess it is no affair of mine, but this may be the best chance you will have." With that he got back on his horse and rode away.

The Indians talked excitedly among themselves for awhile, but finally the crowd broke up and they went back to their own private affairs. That night Isaac lay awake for a long time thinking about all that had happened, and he wondered if he had done the right thing, or if he had been a fool for not going away with the soldier.

Chapter 16

For two days they stayed in the camp. By the third day, however, Cherry Blossom couldn't hold out any longer and decided to go as far as the edge of the town. She was extra watchful that Isaac didn't have a chance to talk to any white people. They didn't visit any of the stores or even walk in the busy section. Instead, they joined a group of jabbering Indian women who were clustered in the shade of the stockade wall.

Isaac was soon bored by the squaws' chatter. The morning dragged for there was nothing to do. When he strayed too far Cherry Blossom would cry out, "Niconza, come back. Don't go away."

For awhile he amused himself by throwing rocks at some blackbirds. Finally he did manage to get to the water's edge without being called back. No one was on the beach, so he sat down alone and watched the little foam-edged waves roll in and flatten out on the sand. The summer sky overhead was a lazy blue, but big white marshmallows of cloud piled against the far horizon. Seagulls wheeled and dipped in search of their dinners. The brown cabins that formed the main part of the town looked as if they were about to be pushed into the lake by the steep, pine covered hill that rose up behind them. The three sailing ships were still tied to the dock. Their straight black masts stood up against the sky like a little grove of bare, branchless trees. He could just make out the name NANCY JANE painted on the prow of the nearest one. Several sailors were on the deck busy with their ship chores. One climbed a rope ladder to a high cross arm and adjusted some of the lashings on the tightly furled sails. Isaac was fascinated by the ships and tried to imagine what it would be like to ride on one.

After awhile a man came off the NANCY JANE. He stopped on

the dock and leisurely lit a pipe, and then started walking along the beach. As he came nearer, Isaac could see that he was a short, stocky man with a monstrous red beard that covered almost his whole face. He walked with a rolling gait and his gold braided cap sat at a jaunty angle.

Suddenly a wonderful idea struck Isaac. He turned to see what Cherry Blossom was doing. At that moment she was happily engrossed in the women's gossip, and she was sitting with her back to him. As the man came near. Isaac spoke to him in a low voice so that the squaws would not hear.

"Excuse me sir," he said. "Are you the captain of that ship?"

"Why yes, laddie," replied the man in a thick Irish brogue. "That I am."

"When will you sail?"

"Well," replied the captain. "With a fresh wind we should be off in the mornin'. But you're askin' a lot of questions, boy."

"Well sir," said Isaac hesitantly. "I'm a captive of the Indians . . ."

"Are you now?" interrupted the Captain. "Why yes, I can see now that you have white features. In those clothes and with that brown skin I thought at first you were one of the Indians."

"No sir," said Isaac. "I'm white, and I'm awfully anxious to get back to my people. I was wondering, sir, if I can run away from the Indians, can I come on your ship and go away with you?"

His heart was pounding with excitement as this new plan of escape began to develop. The captain took his pipe out from between his teeth and spat, and then took a long draw that sent up a cloud of blue-white smoke.

"Now I wouldn't mind helpin' you out lad, but if I was to take you away from your Indian folks it would cause a mighty big ruckus, that's for sure. You see I have to depend on these Indians for my business, so . . ."

"But sir," argued Isaac, "maybe they wouldn't know it was you that took me away."

"Maybe they wouldn't, and then again maybe they would," said the captain, shrugging. "I can't take a chance of startin' a fight between the whites and the reds. Things is bad enough now."

The next moment Isaac heard Cherry Blossom screaming at him. His spirits fell. She had just noticed that he was talking to the captain and she came running and shouting, "Niconza! Niconza! Come! Come at once!"

The captain shifted his cap and started to move on. As he left he whispered. "If you decide to run away lad, be careful how you come. Be real careful."

All the rest of the day Cherry Blossom was very cross. Her mood was as black as the thunderstorm that was brewing in the northwest. Even back in the camp she kept a close watch over Isaac to make sure that he didn't for one moment get out of her sight. All the while his brain was in a whirl. The possibility of escape had always excited him, but this seemed the very best chance he had ever had. "If I can only get to that ship before it sails," he kept telling himself.

There was also a possibility to face. "What will they do to me if I try to escape and they catch me?" he asked himself. "They'll probably beat me or something like that," he decided, "but they won't kill me, that's almost for sure, because Cherry Blossom likes me too well for that."

The sky grew blacker and blacker in the west as the storm came on. When the wind stopped, the air was so still and heavy that the leaves hung limp and motionless on the trees. Deep throated thunder grumbled in the distance. Cherry Blossom was nervous and fretful. "Why don't One Bear come home?" she complained. "There's no reason for him to stay in the town so long. Niconza, come inside."

"I don't want to," Isaac answered. "It's too hot in there. I want to sit out here and watch the lightning."

His mind was full of plans. He turned over one idea after another, wondering all the while if any of them would work. "I've just got to be on that ship when it sails," he said to himself.

A great barbed sword of lightning struck through the black clouds, and the thunder answered back with a crash and a rumble that shook the very roots of the forest.

"Niconza, come inside!" screamed Cherry Blossom.

Isaac rose slowly and went into the hut. It was very dark and hot so he sat just inside the door and looked out at the storm. There was another streak of lightning and a clap of thunder that brought the rain drops down. They were big fat drops that rattled among the leaves and speckled the dust in the path, but that was all. The main force of the storm passed out over the lake. Isaac watched the great grey curtain of rain move away in the distance and he could smell the sweet, wet fragrance that drifted back from it.

When the rain passed, the sky grew lighter. Suddenly, in the last moment of the day, the big fiery sun peeped from under the edge of the clouds and set the western sky aflame with red and gold. It was an age old sign that tomorrow would be a fair day.

"With a fair day tomorrow the Nancy Jane will certainly sail," thought Isaac. He looked at Cherry Blossom's bronzed Indian features and her stiff black braids, and he compared them in his mind with the soft pink and white beauty of the beautiful clean lady at the store, the lady with the pale yellow silken hair caught in a bun at the back of her neck. He looked at the brown flat cakes Cherry Blossom was frying on a hot stone, and thought of the fresh, fluffy white bread with butter and berry jam he had eaten in town. Suddenly he was sick of Cherry Blossom and her scolding and her coarse Indian ways.

"I want to go back to my kind of people," he said to himself, almost aloud. "I've just got to get on that ship tonight."

One Bear came home in the twilight. When he stumbled into the hut they could tell in a moment that he had been drinking fire water with the white men in town. Cherry Blossom was furious. Isaac had never heard her berate him so terribly. She screamed at him and shook her finger in his face and called him a good-for-nothing. He was too drunk to be moved by her scolding, and promptly went to sleep.

111

Cherry Blossom and Isaac ate their suppers in silence. That night, as the night before, Cherry Blossom made Isaac lie beside her, he on the inside next to the wall. For the first time in a long time he remembered to say his "Now I lay me," and when he finished he ended with, "Dear God, please help me to escape tonight and find my way home."

Of course, he found it impossible to sleep. He wondered if he would ever be able to slip out without waking her, or if she would ever go to sleep at all in the first place.

The hours dragged. Both of them were restless. First one and then the other tossed and turned. One Bear, however, snored blissfully.

By tossing and turning Isaac managed to get on top of his side of the blanket. It would be easier to steal out of bed unnoticed if he didn't have to slide from under the cover.

He waited for what seemed hours and hours. The forest outside was unusually still, no cries of animals or night birds. Inside, the hut was quiet too, except for One Bear's snoring. Cherry Blossom had not yet made any sound to indicate she was sleeping.

Time passes slowly for someone who is waiting and although Isaac thought it must surely be almost morning, it was actually only around midnight when Cherry Blossom began to breathe noisily, indicating that at last she had fallen asleep. She drew in her breath slowly and exhaled through her parted lips with a splutter.

Isaac listened for several minutes. The loudest noise he heard was his own pulse throbbing in his ears. Holding his breath, he raised up slowly on his elbow . . . then into a sitting position . . . and waited. Slowly he arose to his feet . . . and waited again. Nothing happened. He stepped lightly across Cherry Blossom and tip-toed as slowly and carefully as he could toward the door. Just as he stooped to go out she suddenly floundered on her bed and changed the tempo of her breathing.

"Dear God, she is waking up," he thought. He was frozen in his tracks and great beads of perspiration popped out on his forehead. "What shall I do? If she catches me now I will never be able to get to the ship tonight."

But Cherry Blossom did not awaken, and in a moment she resumed her steady breathing. He slipped through the door and ran on tip-toe toward the lake as fast as he could.

All the other huts were silent. Not even a dog was aroused. The sky was full of faraway stars, but it was a dark night. He paused again to listen. He heard nothing.

When he came to the lake's edge the water looked black and limitless. The little waves went plop, plop on the shore, and everything seemed unreal and out of proportion in the darkness. He selected a small bark canoe and quickly pulled it into the water. It made a thunderous noise as it scraped on the sand.

Once afloat, he worked the paddle with all his strength. As the shore began to slip away behind, the forest became a black indistinct smear in the darkness. He strained his eyes to try to see if anyone had followed him to the beach, but he couldn't see anything. He paddled as fast as he could in the direction of the town where the ships were moored. It seemed a long, long way in the darkness, much further than it had seemed in the daytime, but finally he could make out the dim silhouettes of the tall masts against the starlit sky and the hulk of the NANCY JANE began to take shape.

When the canoe slipped into shallow water along the beach and ground to a jolting stop on the sand, he jumped out and started to run toward the big ship. But he had gone only a few steps when he stopped short in his tracks as the thought came to him, "If One Bear and Cherry Blossom follow me they will certainly find the canoe and know for sure that I have come here. I must do something with the canoe."

First he thought he would set it adrift, but on the other hand he knew it would probably float back to the shore some place close by, so he gave up that idea. Finally he decided to drag it out of the water to a clump of thick bushes on the shore and hide it beneath some low branches.

A solitary dog barked in the village. As he walked back

toward the NANCY JANE he felt very small and lonely in the great indefinite expanse of the night's blackness.

"What if the captain won't take me aboard?" he suddenly thought, and he was frightened.

He cautiously approached the plank that led from the wharf to the deck. Everything was very quiet and dark except a small feeble lantern that glimmered faintly on the forward deck.

He set his foot upon the plank and stopped to listen and look. He heard nothing and saw no one. Almost on tip-toe he started to creep up the steep incline. It was hard to keep balance on the narrow plank in the dark. His heart was pounding like a hammer.

"Holy Mother o' God," boomed a voice in the darkness, "It's the captive boy after all."

Isaac was so startled that he almost jumped right off the plank into the water. He hadn't seen Captain O'Connor standing by the rail in the shadows.

"Welcome aboard, son."

"Thank you sir," replied Isaac weakly. He was shaking like a leaf. "It's real good of you."

"I couldn't sleep for thinkin' o' you, lad," said the captain. "But I'd just about given you up. Are you bein' followed?"

"I don't think so," stammered Isaac. "I slipped out while they were asleep."

"Well it's right glad I am that you made it, boy, but them Indians are sure to come a-lookin' for you, and there still may be the devil to pay. Come below, lad, and I'll see what can be done to stow you away."

The captain brought the lantern from the forward deck and led the way down some steep stairs into the dark, musty inside of the ship.

They came to a door so low it made them stoop to get through. Inside seemed to be a sort of storeroom, for there were piles of boxes and bundles and barrels. A negro boy was fast asleep in a bunk bed built beside the wall. The captain held the lantern high and shook him vigorously.

114

"Nicodemus!" he boomed. "Nicodemus! Hear me boy. Wake up!"

The negro turned lazily on his bed, and his lids slowly parted showing the great whites of his eyes.

"Come boy, on your feet," cried the captain. "Wake up so you can understand what I'm about to say to you."

The sleepy boy yawned and staggered to his feet. He was scarcely taller than Isaac. His skin was very black and the whites of his eyes so very white that they shown almost like lights in the half darkness.

"What you all want wid me, mistuh captain?" he stammered.

"Nicodemus, listen to me boy," said the captain. "Are you full awake so you can understand what I want you to do?"

"Yes suh, I is woke up."

"Then listen to me. This boy here," continued the captain, laying his hand on Isaac's shoulder, "has run away from the Indians. We're going to stow him away until after we sail in the morning. If the Indians come here to look for him, which I don't doubt they will, you're to hide him away in some safe place and swear you haven't seen a white boy on this ship, understand? You'll have plenty of time to hide him when you hear 'em come topside."

"Yes suh, I understands," Nicodemus assured him.

"Be bloomin' sure you do. And do exactly what I've told you," warned the captain, "or I'll lay it on your hide in the morning."

"Yes suh!"

"Now you lads better get some sleep," said the captain, and with that he turned and left them.

When the lantern was gone it was inky black. Nicodemus yawned loudly and fumbled his way back into his bed. "You all can lay down here too if you wants to," he said.

Isaac felt his way to the bunk and stretched out his tired body beside the negro boy. It was good to rest.

Nicodemus was soon fast asleep again, but Isaac lay awake

and stared into the darkness and strained his ears for sounds. He heard a rat gnawing its way into the cargo, and he heard the creaking of the timbers in the ship's structure, but everything else was still. The air was hot and heavy. The hours dragged. Finally, completely exhausted from all the excitement, his eyelids fell shut. Without intending to, he drifted away into a deep sleep.

"White boy! White boy! You all better wake up!"

Isaac came awake with a start. It was broad daylight. For a moment he couldn't think where he was. Nicodemus's black face was bending over him and he saw fright in the big white eyes.

"You all better get up outa dat bed," cried the negro boy. "There's Indians top side."

Isaac sprang to his feet. Now he could hear the commotion overhead . . . voices that were both angry and excited. He was sure that the shrill, high voice was Cherry Blossom's. Then he could hear the deep voice of the captain answer in an angry tone. He couldn't make out the words they were saying, but he could tell there was a serious argument going on.

"Quick, where can I hide?" cried Isaac. "They may come down here any minute."

"I done fix you a place whilst you was sleepin'," answered Nicodemus. "Climb over dem boxes and you find an empty barrel behind them. You get you'self in dat barrel and I pile mo' truck on top of you, and they'll never find you."

Isaac hurried to get into his hiding place, and he was not a bit too soon. Nicodemus had hardly put the last of the boxes in place when they heard the voices coming down the stairs.

"You can search the ship from stem to stern if you're a mind to," cried the captain angrily, "but you'll find no Indian boy here."

"I tell you he is no Indian boy," screamed Cherry Blossom. "he is really a white boy, but he is our son. We have made his adoption. He is my Niconza, and I want you to give him back."

"What makes you think I've got your Niconza, or whatever you call him?" snapped the captain.

116

"We found his canoe hid in the bushes," said One Bear. "We think he came to this ship."

"Well have a look around, if that's what you want to do," said the captain. "But hurry it up, I've got work to do."

When Cherry Blossom first saw Nicodemus she started to grab him, for she thought for a moment it was Isaac who had painted his face black to trick her, but she soon saw her mistake. Nicodemus, his eyes big as saucers, insisted he had seen no one as the captain had warned him.

It was hot in the barrel, but Isaac sat very still and tried to breathe as little as possible.

Cherry Blossom was nearly in tears. He could tell from the sound of her voice. "I know you have my Niconza," she cried, "and I want you to give him back."

"Look," said the captain, irritated. "Why do you pick on *me*? What makes you think it's me that's got the boy? The ship NORTH STAR that was tied next to me sailed before dawn. Maybe he went off on her."

There was a silence. "That is true," said One Bear to Cherry Blossom. "There was another ship here yesterday."

That thought dampened the argument.

"If you had been content to stay where you belong, with the women of your family back at the village, this would not have happened," said One Bear sullenly.

After awhile the voices died away and Isaac knew they had gone above and finally left the ship.

When at last he came out of his hiding the NANCY JANE was underway. When he went up onto the deck the cool, sweet breeze struck his nostrils, refreshing after the stuffy air below. The great white sails overhead were fat with wind, and the island of Mackinac was drifting away in the distance behind them.

Isaac walked to the rail and looked down into the deep blue water. It was far bluer than the morning sky above. He felt the gentle motion of the ship. The fresh wind blew in his hair, and he had such a sense of freedom and joy that he almost wanted to dance and sing.

The captain came up and leaned on the rail beside him. "Well lad, we made it," he said. "That squaw gave me a might of back talk, but I finally persuaded her. Good thing the NORTH STAR sailed before us. I made 'em believe that you had gone off on her."

"Yes," replied Isaac. "I could hear everything you said. Thank you for all you've done for me."

"Tis nothing, lad, nothing at all. I'm glad I could help you get your freedom."

"Where are we heading?" asked Isaac suddenly. He had been so intent on escape that it hadn't even occurred to him to think where he was going.

"Detroit," replied the captain.

Isaac didn't know where Detroit was, but he was sure he was on his way home, so he didn't question it.

The days on shipboard were a delight. He never tired of watching the sailors at their work. They made him tell them over and over again all the adventures he had had with the Indians. In fact, he became a favorite of every man in the crew. One sailor, who knew something of tailoring, remade an old pair of trousers and a shirt so that he would have something proper to wear when they got to Detroit. When he took off his Indian clothes and dressed in his new ones he thought, "It's good to be a white boy again."

Chapter 17

In 1794 Detroit was a growing frontier city of some three hundred buildings. There were a few farms scattered up and down the river, but most of the houses were clustered around Fort Lernoult, which at that time was occupied by the British.

When the NANCY JANE slid up beside the wharf, Isaac was

standing on the deck amazed at the sight that spread before his eyes. He had never seen such a city before with so many houses and such a bustle of activity. Wharf hands were loading kegs and barrels onto wagons, and there were great heaps of boxes and bags piled everywhere along the waterfront where the tall masted sailing ships were moored. There were crowds of people in the streets. Beyond the fort, a platoon of red-coated soldiers paraded on a green meadow.

He watched it all with great interest and excitement at first. Then suddenly he realized that the voyage was done and he would soon have to go ashore. Already it was late afternoon, and he wondered where he could go that night in such a big city. It was puzzling, and he admitted to himself that he was a little frightened at the prospect. While leaning on the rail occupied with these thoughts, the captain came up and put his arm around his shoulders.

"And now that we have arrived, where will you be goin' lad?"

"I guess I'll head right on for Kentucky," said Isaac rather uncertainly, for he didn't even have the slightest idea in which direction Kentucky lay.

"Well now," said the captain with a smile and a wink of his eye, "that'll be a bit of a journey. I think you had better have some supper with me first, lad. It's always better, you know, to start off on a journey with a full stomach."

"I sure want to thank you sir," said Isaac, "for bringing me with you on your ship."

"Now don't mention it boy," replied the captain.

When the ship was finally secured, they went ashore. By then the sun had set. They strode across the wharf and along the waterfront street that was still busy with pedestrians and horsemen and dogs that scurried along in the deepening twilight. The captain shouted greetings to old friends here and there. The shop keepers began to light their lanterns.

When they came to a building that had a big swinging signboard outside painted CAFE EDMOND, the captain stopped and gave his trousers a hitch.

"Hungry lad?" he asked smiling down at Isaac.

"Yes sir, a little."

"Then let's eat."

The CAFE EDMOND was owned by a Frenchman named Edmond Risseau. He had remained in the city after the fort fell from France into the hands of the British. It was a warm, friendly place where everyone gathered for good food and good conversation. When they entered they found the tables were nearly all filled. There were red-coated soldiers, seamen, dock workers, travelers, and men from the city. The room hummed with talk and the air was warm and heavily scented with the good odors of food. As they passed among the crowded tables Captain O'Connor greeted one or two acquaintances who were already seated.

"Ah—zee Cap-i-tan O'Connor!" cried a cheery voice with a heavy French accent. "It ees good to have you back! Welcome once again to zee Cafe Edmond." It was the proprietor, Monsieur Risseau, who rushed up to welcome them with a broad smile and a warm handshake.

"Good to see you again, Eddie," replied the captain. "You know I always come to your place when I'm in Detroit. What's for supper?"

"Ah, my friend, I have zee good onion soup tonight and zee beef roast. It ees very good. Come I will sit you down." And he hurried to make a place for them. "Ees this your little boy?" he asked, smiling at Isaac.

"Well . . . yes and no," replied the captain, chuckling. "I kind of picked him up at Mackinac. He's been a captive of the Indians and he ran away."

"Ah, zee pauvre!" cried the innkeeper, patting Isaac on the shoulder. "Eddie will fix for you a very special supper."

As he hustled away into the kitchen, Isaac decided at once that he liked the man. He was amused by the funny accent, and he liked the friendly smile and the merry twinkle in his eyes.

"I think this is the place where we may find help for you," said the captain.

120

When their host returned a few minutes later he carried a huge bowl of hot onion soup in each hand and a loaf of dark bread under his arm.

"There!" he cried, placing the bowls and bread before them. "It ees Eddie's specialty . . . it ees good, no?"

The soup was delicious. Isaac thought he had never tasted anything to quite equal it. "I like this," he said enthusiastically, when he had put the first steaming spoonful in his mouth.

"Then you have made me very happy. Good appetite."

"Eddie," said the captain, "you know everybody in Detroit. I'm thinking you're just the man that might be able to help us."

"Ah . . . cap-i-tan," replied the Frenchman with a friendly twinkle in his eye. "It would make me a great pleasure to be of service to my good friend. What can I do for you?"

"The boy here," continued the captain, "has been a captive of the Indians for a long time, and now he's anxious to get back to his father and mother in Kentucky as soon as he can."

"Ah, le pauvre. Of course he ees."

"Who do you know in Detroit that might be traveling to that country?"

The Frenchman tilted his head back and stroked his chin in thought. "I know no one here from Kentucky," he replied. "There was a man last spring, but he has gone away."

"I'll be sailing again in a few days," continued the captain, "and I'd like to see the lad in good hands before I leave. I had thought of turning him over to the British garrison. They would feed him well, I have no doubt of that. But as you know, the English and the Americans are not too friendly, so I doubt if they would make any effort to send him home."

Eddie ran his fingers through his black, curly hair and scratched his head. Suddenly there was a flash of inspiration on his face. "Ah," he cried. "It comes to me now. They say there ees many soldiers from Kentucky with the American General Wayne at Grand Glaize. They call them Kentucky Volunteers. I know well a man named Roger Pea who will go

121

soon to Grand Glaize. He was in my cafe last night. Maybe he comes again tonight. I will watch for him."

"Eddie, you are a good friend," replied the captain. "I knew I could depend on you. Find this Roger Pea and see if he will take the boy to General Wayne."

Edmond Risseau hurried away to wait on his other customers. Isaac and the captain resumed their meal. The food was excellent, and Isaac ate and ate until he couldn't possibly force down another mouthful.

The captain joined in conversation with the other men in the cafe. All the talk was of a great victory that General Wayne had just won over the Indians at a place called the Fallen Timbers. The battle had occurred only the week before on August 20th at a place where many trees had been uprooted by a cyclone. The Indians had thought to use the fallen trees as cover during the battle, but their plans had failed.

"They tell me the fighting didn't last more than an hour," said one man.

"Never saw Indians yet that could stand up under a bayonet attack," said another.

"Blue Jacket spread his warriors in too thin a line. The way I hear it, he was going to try to outflank Wayne's legion and got cut right down the middle instead."

"That Anthony Wayne is a smart general."

"He's a tough one, that's for sure. They say his gout was so bad that his men had to lift him into the saddle the morning of the battle, but he never quits when there's a skirmish."

"I hear they're calling him Tornado Wayne now because he went through them Indians like the wind went through the trees last summer."

"How many men did he lose?"

"Not more than twenty dead the way I hear it, but nobody knows how many Indians. They carry them away, you know."

"I heard that the British at Fort Miami were supposed to give the Indians help."

"Help? They wouldn't even open the stockade gate after

the battle was over to let the wounded ones in. I hear that Little Turtle and Blue Jacket beat on the gate and begged Major Campbell to let them come in. He wouldn't even answer them."

"I knew an Indian once who used to say, 'Don't trust the Redcoats. They go back on their word.'"

"Sure looks like they went back on their word this time."

"Well, I guess I shouldn't be saying this right here in the shadow of the British garrison," said one man in a half whisper, "but the day is coming soon, and you can mark my word, when the Americans will take over all this country."

"Wouldn't be at all surprised the way Wayne has been going. He's come all the way up from the Ohio River just since last winter, you know."

"Looks like it'll be the British and the Americans from now on, don't it? Sure don't look like the Indians got much fight left."

Isaac listened to all this talk with interest, but his stomach was full and the room was warm. Finally his eyelids grew heavy and the voices seemed to get farther and farther away. Soon his head fell over on his arms on the table and he was fast asleep.

Bright yellow sunshine was streaming through the window across a gay patchwork quilt when he awoke. He rubbed his eyes and looked about in wonder. Where was this he found himself? He was in a big wooden bed on smooth white sheets in a pleasant little room that smelled of cedar and clean bed clothes. It was like a dream.

He sat upright and looked about. Last night he had eaten supper at the CAFE EDMOND, but he couldn't remember what had happened after that. He was bewildered, but it was a wonderful feeling to find himself once again in a real house. He jumped out of bed and ran to the window. Thin wisps of white smoke trailed from the chimneys of the houses down the street. The morning sky was deep blue. There was a faint smell of bacon frying. It all seemed almost too wonderful to believe.

The bedroom door opened cautiously on a squeaky hinge, and he turned to see the curly black head of his new friend, Edmond Risseau, peeping in through a narrow crack. The Frenchman's face burst into a great smile.

"Ah, bonjour!" he cried, flinging the door wide. "You are already awake. Did you not sleep well?"

"Oh yes," answered Isaac, "I really did, but when I woke up I didn't know where I was."

Monsieur Risseau laughed. "You were so tired last night that you fell asleep at zee table. Your friend, Cap-i-tan O'Connor, and I carried you here and put you in zee bed, and you did not even wake up."

Isaac blushed in embarrassment at the thought of having been carried to bed like a child. He grinned sheepishly and said only, "It was a very good bed."

"Come!" cried the Frenchman. "My wife Marie has made breakfast. We must hurry, for soon zee man, Roger Pea, ees coming to get you. He leaves for Fort Defiance at Grand Glaize this morning, and he will take you to zee American General Wayne."

Isaac jumped into his trousers and followed his friend to the kitchen below.

Marie Risseau was a pretty French woman with smooth dark hair and large eyes.

"Ah, here is our guest," she said smiling, as Isaac entered the room. "Good morning, monsieur. Come and sit down and I will serve you breakfast."

The room smelled good with the odors of cooking. Isaac took the chair she indicated at a table that was spread with a blue checked cloth and set with blue flowered dishes.

"My husband tells me," she continued, "that you have been for a long time a captive of the Indians, so I would like to fix you a very special breakfast today. What would you like?"

Isaac hardly knew what to say. He smiled at Madame Ris-

124

seau. He thought she was very pretty. "Don't go to any trouble on my account," he said.

"Ah, mon cher," she cried. "It ees no trouble. What would you say to some of my fresh biscuits with honey, and some ham, and maybe a big mug of milk?"

Milk! He suddenly remembered he hadn't tasted any for nearly two years. His mouth watered at the thought. "That would be just what I would like," he said.

As the kind lady bustled about her kitchen to serve him, Monsieur Risseau went into the front room to wait on his late customers in the cafe.

"Your mama will be glad to see you," said Madame Risseau.

"Yes," replied Isaac, "and I will be glad to see her. I wonder if she thinks I'm dead?" He didn't know why he had said that. It was the first time such a thought had entered his head.

"Ah, no . . . mamas have a way of knowing about their little boys. I once had a little boy . . . eat your breakfast."

After awhile, just as he was finishing his wonderful meal, Monsieur Risseau came back into the kitchen to announce that Roger Pea had arrived.

"If you have eaten all you can, zee man Roger Pea has come for you," he said. "Monsieur Pea ees anxious to leave at once. Marie, quick . . . fix a lunch for our young friend to take on zee journey."

"Where is Captain O'Connor?" asked Isaac.

"Ah, zee Cap-i-tan O'Connor," replied Monsieur Risseau. "He has gone back to his ship. He said to tell you that he hopes you have a safe and pleasant journey home."

"But I would like to see him and thank him for all he has done for me," insisted Isaac.

"I fear there ees no time for that. Monsieur Pea ees anxious to leave. I will tell zee cap-i-tan when I see him that you send him thanks and farewell."

And so Isaac and the Risseaus left the warm, sweet-smelling kitchen and went out into the street in front of the cafe where Roger Pea sat waiting on a big black horse. When Isaac tried to say thank you and goodbye to his new friends he saw their eyes puddle up with tears. They both gave him a squeeze and a big kiss on each cheek. Madame Risseau tucked a huge bundle of food into the saddle bag.

"This is for the journey," she said. "You must not eat it now."

Then Isaac climbed up behind Roger Pea, and as they rode away he could see the Risseaus waving to him until the horse turned the bend in the street and the CAFE EDMOND disappeared from view.

Chapter 18

The journey to Grand Glaize was pleasant. Roger Pea said he had once lived at Post Vincennes on the Wabash River, which was not a great distance from Isaac's home at the Red Banks. He had studied to be a minister of the gospel and had done some circuit riding in the Wabash and Ohio River valleys.

"I know the Red Banks well," he said. "I preached a sermon there once, but I can't remember having met anyone there named Knight."

Then Isaac told him that his family was new at the Red Banks—that they had moved there only a few days before he was captured. Anyway, even though Roger Pea had not met his parents, Isaac had a good feeling to be with someone who was familiar with his home country. It was next best thing to finding an old friend.

The forest through which they rode was showing the first signs of autumn. Tall goldenrod bordered the trail and nodded dusty, yellow heads as they passed by. There was a loud cawing of crows on the opposite bank of the river. The birds were gathering in great flocks among the highest branches of the trees, for the time was not far off when they would start their flight to the south.

The journey from Detroit to General Wayne's headquarters took three days. They stayed the first night in the cabin of a settler by the shore of Lake Erie. The second night was spent in the forest, sleeping on the new fallen leaves beneath the stars. They talked of many things, and by the time the journey was done they felt as if they had known each other forever.

When they came at last to Fort Defiance at the end of the third day the sun had already set. Once safely inside the stockade the sentinels took charge of the horse and they were taken immediately to the soldiers' quarters where supper was being served. When the men of the Kentucky Volunteers learned that Isaac was from their home country they gathered around him and welcomed him as one of their own. Several of the men went to their knapsacks and hunted out special tidbits they had saved from their rations and gave him.

"Nothing's too good for a boy from Kentucky," someone cried.

Of course they made him tell of his adventures with the Indians. Although he was very tired from the three days' journey on horseback, he sat until late with the men around the campfire and told them many of the things that had happened to him. When he finally rolled himself into blankets the soldiers had given him, he slept so soundly that it was an hour after sun-up next morning before he awoke.

"Thought you maybe died," said one of the soldiers jokingly. "Never seen a boy sleep so sound with the sun a-shining in his face."

"I guess I was pretty tired," said Isaac yawning.

"Yep, you been through a heap for a boy your size. You had the rest comin'. Bet your maw and paw will shore be glad to see you. You say you're from the Red Banks?"

"Yes," said Isaac. "We moved down there from the Green River just before I was caught by the Indians."

127

"You wouldn't have knowed some folks thereabouts by the name of Sprinkle would you? They had a boy that was killed by the Indians."

"Sure I know them," cried Isaac. "I was with the Sprinkle boys when Peter Sprinkle was killed. He and Jacob Upp both got scalped. The rest of us got carried away."

"Is that a fact!" cried the soldier in amazement. "Jumpin' Jehosophat, now ain't that a coincidence. I knowed there was some other boys mixed up in that fracas, but I never learned their names, and I shore didn't take you to be one of them. Hey, Andy." He called to another soldier on the other side of the courtyard. "This here boy was with the Sprinkle boy when he got scalped."

The soldier named Andy sauntered over. "Is that a fact?" he drawled, and spat a long squirt of tobacco juice. "You been with the Injuns ever since?"

"Yes," said Isaac, "until about a month ago when I ran away. Do you know anything about my folks?" he asked eagerly.

"Your name's Knight you say?"

"Yes sir."

"Never knowed the Knights. You see I ain't never lived at the Red Banks myself, but I knowed all about the Sprinkle boy because the Sprinkles was sort of kinfolks of mine. His maw shore took it hard."

"His brother, George, was a prisoner with me for awhile," said Isaac. "But we got separated after a couple or three weeks. I wonder whatever happened to him?"

"Oh, I hear tell the little Sprinkle boy come back home after a spell. Course I don't know for sure, but leastways that's what I heard."

By now the cooks were calling to Isaac to come and get his breakfast before they washed up the kettles. Most of the soldiers had finished eating. Many of them had already begun their day's work. There had been no active war with the Indians since the battle of Fallen Timbers, so the troops were mostly assigned to camp duties when they weren't on watch. Some were digging the trenches deeper and wider and building up tremendous earthworks. Others were repairing the stockade wall. In general they were being kept busy making the fort more solid and comfortable before the winter weather set in.

While Isaac was eating his breakfast a neatly dressed soldier came up looking for him.

"Are you the boy that arrived last night who has been a captive of the Indians?" he asked politely.

"Yes sir," replied Isaac.

"General Wayne would like to see you in his office as soon as possible," said the soldier.

"Jumpin' Jehosophat!" cried one of the cooks who had overheard. "You better wash up good, boy, before you go in to see Old Hoss. He's perticular."

Old Hoss was a nickname the soldiers used when they spoke of General Wayne behind his back. That name, and the cook's warning, struck a cold fear into Isaac. He gulped down the rest of his breakfast and hurried to the well to draw a bucket of water to wash himself. He scrubbed his hands and face carefully, even behind his ears, and then wet down his hair and smoothed it with his hands.

His heart was thumping with nervous excitement when he came to the building where the General was waiting. He had never met such an important person before, and he was not sure how he was supposed to act. He wondered if he should salute when he entered the room. He tucked his shirt more neatly into the top of his trousers and smoothed his hair once again.

"I have been told to come to see the General," he said to the sentinel at the door.

The soldier was in full uniform and carried a musket. He stood very tall and stiff. When he spoke, his voice was sharp and matter of fact.

"Follow me. The General is waiting for you," he said.

Isaac was getting very nervous. He followed the soldier into the building and along a hall to a doorway where the soldier snapped to stiff attention and saluted.

"The boy who escaped from the Indians to see the General, sir," he announced.

A big voice boomed out from within the room, "Bring him in."

Isaac wished at that moment that the floor would open and swallow him up, but the soldier took him by the arm and pushed him through the door.

There the great Anthony Wayne sat sideways at his desk with one foot swathed in bandages and propped up on a stool. He had been suffering a great deal lately with the gout. His face was stern and his eyes piercing, but in spite of that there was a small spark of kindness there. His skin was brown and tough-looking like leather from too much sun and wind. It looked especially dark in contrast to his white powdered wig which sat somewhat askew at the moment. The desk was littered with papers, and there was a horn of ink and some quill pens lying about, for the general had been preparing despatches to be sent out with the next courier.

"So you're the boy that was captured by the Indians?"

"Yes sir." Isaac thought he sounded very high and squeaky as compared to the big voice of the general.

"Well come in, lad. Let's have a talk. I'm not going to bite you. Tell me your name."

Isaac took a small step forward and swallowed. "Isaac Knight," he said very weakly.

"Isaac Knight, eh? Isaac's a good name. My father's name was Isaac . . . a good Christian name. Step closer, boy."

Isaac advanced another step, and began to feel a bit easier in the General's presence.

"Tell me, Isaac, all you can about the activities of the tribes. What have you seen?"

"I'm afraid I don't know what you mean, sir," said Isaac.

"Then let me say it this way," continued General Wayne. "My business here is to clear this territory of the Indians and make it safe for our people to colonize. We have just scored a decisive victory at Fallen Timbers, but nobody knows when or where we will encounter the savages again. Anything you can tell me about the war activities of the tribes, or their strength, the preparations they are making, or even what they are saying might be a great help to me and to our country."

Isaac saw now the purpose and the importance of this interview, and he tried to think back to the things he had seen and heard. For a brief moment he imagined himself the great hero who came through with the vital information from the enemy, but unfortunately nothing he could remember seemed very important. He remembered the twelve warriors who had gone away to war from the village of Cherry Blossom's people, and he told that to the general. Then he tried to think of things he had heard the Indians say as he listened to their talk around the camp fires.

"I think sir," he said at last, "that the Indians are mainly afraid of you. They talk a great deal about having to give up their lands. I believe they fear you very much, for I often heard them mention your name."

"But you have seen no great concentrations of warriors, or great war dances?"

"No sir, nothing like that."

"Well, I didn't really expect that you would have any information that would be useful to us," said the General. "But I always check every possibility."

Isaac was disappointed that he wasn't able to be more helpful. "My Indian father was an Ottawa and a fur trader," he said apologetically, "not a warrior. He wasn't interested much in fighting. The Potowatamies, that I lived with first, got the smallpox and almost all of them died."

"Ah," said the General, "that disease is one of our greatest allies. The Indians have no resistance to it whatsoever. I have seen whole tribes wiped out in a few weeks." General Wayne painfully changed the position of his bandaged foot so as to rest it a bit. "I guess your main concern now, Isaac, is to get home, isn't it?" he said.

"Yes sir," said Isaac. "I want to get home as soon as I can."

"Corporal!" shouted the General. The soldier appeared at the door. "Corporal, I want this lad sent south with the supply train tomorrow. Who will be in charge of the wagons?"

"Lieutenant Watson, Sir."

"Tell Watson he is to take good care of this boy. When they get to Cincinnati he is to be directly responsible for seeing that the lad gets transportation on a boat going down river."

"Yes, sir!"

"And corporal, see to it yourself that enough extra rations are drawn to do him while he's with the wagon train."

"Yes, sir."

"Tell Lieutenant Watson to see me before he leaves in the morning. I think I had better give him the full instructions myself. That is all."

The Corporal saluted and left the room.

General Wayne leaned across his desk and looked straight into Isaac's eyes. Then he extended his hand and said kindly, "Isaac, you're a fine lad. I wish you a safe journey home."

Isaac felt the strong warm grip of the great soldier's handshake.

"Thank you, sir," he said proudly. "But I'm sorry I couldn't give you more information about the Indians."

"That's all right, my boy. We'll make out."

Isaac felt certain they would.

"Now out with you," said the General. "I have work to do."

Chapter 19

Isaac felt that at last he was really on his way home. He began to count the days. The men on the wagon train said it would take at least a week of actual traveling to reach Cincinnati, but enroute they would stop for two or three days at Fort Greenville to rest the horses.

"About ten days then," he thought, "and I will see the big river again."

The hours seemed to drag by, but finally the days dwindled down to seven, then to six. He kept track by cutting a notch in the wagon seat every night when the caravan stopped. There were fifteen wagons in all. They were mostly empty because they were going to pick up winter supplies for the garrison, but even empty as they were traveling was slow. When the General advanced north he had cut a road through the forest, but all it actually amounted to was clearing a wide trail. All the trees and brush had been cut out, but the stumps still stood up in the way so that the wagons had to zig-zag continually to keep from running into them. They forded the streams, but often that caused a lot of trouble and delay. Sometimes a wagon would strike soft sand in a creek bed and sink up to the hubs. Then everybody had to stop and lend a hand to pry it out.

It was also necessary to keep a watch out at all times for hostile Indians. Although the back of the Indian resistance had been broken at the battle of Fallen Timbers, there were still wandering bands of warriors who were daring enough to attack a wagon train to get the horses, if nothing more. So guards were on duty night and day and every man kept his musket ready.

One night in the forest they heard the hooting of an owl that sounded strangely human. Some of the men were certain that the call was a signal from Indians lying in ambush. Almost everybody in camp stayed awake and watchful all night, but nothing happened.

They stopped for two days at Fort Greenville as they had planned. The fort itself was much like Fort Defiance, but more strongly fortified, for it had been established longer. There were more log buildings inside the compound, the trenches were deeper and wider, and the earthworks higher. Isaac was impressed in a way, but he had had so much of traveling and adventure by this time that his main thoughts were of getting home as quickly as possible.

133

Finally, having rested, the train pushed on, and after several more days they came to Fort Washington just outside Cincinnati. The very next morning Lieutenant Watson took Isaac into town, as the General had instructed him to do, to try to find passage for him on a flat boat.

Cincinnati was a brawling town of red painted frame buildings that sprawled along the river bank. There were several boats tied up there, so it wasn't hard to find someone who would agree to take on another passenger, especially after they had heard Isaac's story.

The family with whom he sailed was named Stafford. They were English folks who had come out of Pennsylvania to settle in the Ohio valley wilderness. They were very kind and pleasant to Isaac, and required nothing of him, so all he had to do during the rest of the journey was sit in the sun all day and whittle and watch the densely forested river banks glide by. It was now mid-October and the weather was clear and crisp. The trees were taking on the brilliant reds and golds of autumn. Sometimes he would see deer at the water's edge, but they would bound away into the forest when they got scent of the boat. It was wonderful and beautiful, but the days passed too slowly.

Finally, at the very end of the month, the scenery began to seem more familiar. When they passed what he was certain was the mouth of the Green River he became tense with excitement and anticipation. He stood at the very front of the boat and scanned both banks for any certain landmarks. They rounded a great horseshoe bend in the river which he seemed to remember. And then, sure enough, there was the giant, white-barked sycamore tree which they had used as a mark on that fateful day when the boys crossed over to the cane brake. There was no mistaking it. Yes, he was home at last. There, over the trees, was the thin blue smoke from the chimneys of the Red Banks settlement.

"You are certain," said Mr. Stafford, "that this is the place?"

"Yes, yes," cried Isaac, jumping up and down, "I can see my house now. See . . . there it is," and he tried to point it out.

He couldn't help noticing, however, that many changes had taken place while he had been gone. Several new houses had been built, and a lot more of the forest had been cleared away. Where the thicket had been at the top of the path there was a field with long rows of rusty, brown corn shocks and piles of big yellow pumpkins. At that very moment a tall, thin boy was carrying a big pumpkin up from the far end of the field.

"Now if you are certain this is the right settlement," said Mr. Stafford, "I will put you ashore."

"Oh, yes sir!" cried Isaac. "I am sure."

So Mr. Stafford put out a skiff, and in a few minutes Isaac was once again standing on the good soil of Kentucky.

When the boy with the pumpkin saw that someone had come off the boat he came running out of the field and down the path. As he and Isaac got closer together they both stopped dead still in their tracks and stared at each other. Gradually a smile of surprise and recognition broke on both their faces.

"Isaac!"

"John!"

They both cried in unison and rushed together and threw their arms about each other in a big, brotherly bear hug. Then John pushed Isaac back and held him by the shoulders at arms' length to look at him better.

"I didn't hardly recognize you, brother," he cried. "You're a whole head taller and you've sure changed. Where you been, boy? We thought you was a goner for sure."

"I've been a far piece," replied Isaac. "But it's sure good to be back. How's our mother?"

"Oh, ma's fine, but wait till she learns you're back. Hey, come on. I'll race you up to the house."

The boys broke into a run, John in the lead, shouting at the top of his voice, "Ma! Oh, ma! Come see who's here!"

Mrs. Knight appeared in the door shaking flour from her apron. She shaded her eyes with her hands to see what all the commotion was about.

"Ma!" cried John. "Look who's here!"

The boys raced up to the cabin door all out of breath. At first glance Mrs. Knight didn't even recognize Isaac, but when he smiled and started to speak she clamped her hands to her cheeks in wide-eyed, open-mouthed surprise. Then, with a little cry, she ran to clasp him in her arms. For a long moment neither spoke a word, but the tears welled up and trickled down their faces.

"Oh my son, my son," she sobbed, twining her fingers in his hair and pressing his head hard to her bosom. "You've come home safe."

They both burst into tears of sheer joy.

"John," she said, sniffling. "Run quick into the fields and fetch your father and your brother Joshua. And the other children, too, who are herding the cows."

"Oh mother, I've missed you so much," whispered Isaac, hugging her again. "And I'm so glad to be home."

They both cried some more.

Word spread quickly through the settlement that the Knights' boy, who had been captured by the Indians, had come home. It was the only topic of conversation for the rest of the afternoon. When evening came, the neighbors began to gather from far and near to see Isaac and to welcome him back.

Among the guests were George Sprinkle and John Upp. He was glad to see them again and learn that they had really come home safely as the soldier at Fort Defiance had told him.

"How long you been back?" he asked.

"Oh, we been back more'n a year now," boasted George. "We were only gone about five months—met up with some white scouts that took us away from the Indians."

"Last time I saw you," said Isaac, "you were all togged out and painted up like Indians and stepping high with the squaws in a circle dance."

136

George got red in the face and everybody laughed.

In those days neighborhood gatherings usually combined work with fun, so it wasn't long until the company began to collect in the barn, and before the evening was over the welcome home party turned into a husking bee. As the men, women, and children all sat around on the barn floor tearing the fat, golden ears from the brown shucks, they begged Isaac to tell them everything that had happened to him. He tried to tell them all he could remember, but strangely he found that being home with his folk was so natural that memories of his life with the Indians seemed to fade away into the far distant past. He wondered, almost, if all the things he was saying had actually happened to him, or had he dreamed some of them.

He told them how Yellow Jacket had cared for him when he was sick with smallpox.

He told about Yellow Jacket's death and funeral, and how, after that, he had been made to work hard when the epidemic raged out of control in the village. Everyone was aghast at his account of his narrow escape from being burned alive.

He described his adoption by One Bear and Cherry Blossom, and told about traveling with them on the big lake that was so big you couldn't even see the land on the other side.

He described the big ships at Mackinac, and told how he had run away at night to get aboard the NANCY JANE with Captain O'Connor.

He told of spending the night at the Cafe Edmond in Detroit, and of the kindness of Eddie and Madame Risseau.

He gave them news of the great battle of Fallen Timbers where the Indians had been overcome, and when he told them that he had actually seen and talked with the great General Anthony Wayne, everybody was amazed and very proud and impressed that their local boy had had the honor to talk to such a great man.

The evening passed quickly. When everyone was tired of husking, the women opened the lunch baskets they had brought. They were brimming with rich, spicy pumpkin pies and big, red-cheeked apples, biscuits spread with wild grape jelly, and home-made cheese and smoked ham. As they ate, the oil lanterns cast a soft yellow glow on the circle of happy and contented faces. It was a wonderful party.

Pretty soon Grandpa Whittlesea brought out his squeaky, old fiddle and struck up a tune. That was invitation enough for the dancers. Around and around they went with a do-si-do to the tunes of *Turkey In The Straw* and *Sourwood Mountain*.

Noah Maltby, who always called the squares, had a reputation for making up clever little songs as he went along. This night was certainly no exception for while the fiddle swang through the melody of Old Joe Clark he began to sing:

"There were five boys from Red Banks town,
I'll tell you of their plight.
Their names were Peter, George and John
And Jake and Isaac Knight.

They crossed the river to cut some cane
One sunny April morning,
But the murderous Indians struck them down
Without a word of warning.

Chorus:
     Isaac Knight was a brave, brave boy
     But they carried him away.
     Then he ran off from the Indians' camp
    And came back home to stay.

Oh what a cruel thing they did
On that fine April day.
They killed and scalped two fine brave lads
And carried three away.

Up through the forest dark and wild

138

'Twas the Potowatamie
That took our Isaac boy away,
Far to the north countree.

Chorus:
> Isaac Knight was a brave, brave boy
> But they carried him away.
> Then he ran off from the Indians' camp
> And came back home to stay.

Over the lake in a bark canoe
To the Isle of Mackinac,
Where he found the good ship, Nancy Jane,
That brought him sailing back.

He met the great man, Tony Wayne,
To whom we owe much thanks,
For sending Isaac straight way home
To us here on Red Banks.

Pretty soon everybody began to catch on to the song, and each time he came to the chorus they would all join in:

Isaac Knight was a brave, brave boy
But they carried him away.
Then he ran off from the Indians' camp
And came back home to stay.

When the song was all done there was plenty of laughter and applause.

It was just about the most wonderful homecoming party anybody ever had.

Since that happy night, the years have come and gone until more than a century and a half has passed, but Isaac has not been forgotten even yet. On the walls of the Evansville

Soldiers' and Sailors' Memorial Coliseum there is a mural depicting his capture by the Indians on that day so long ago.

When Isaac grew up to be a man, he crossed the river once again, this time not to cut the cane, but to build a home for his wife and children on a farm that was located at what is now the eastern limits of the City of Evansville, Indiana. In 1815 he became a freeholder and lived on these lands until he died. He did many good and noble works in the community, and today his name is still remembered as the founder of the area called Knight Township.

The Indians, of course, have long since disappeared from the scene, and so has most of the forest, but the great, beautiful Ohio River continues to follow its winding, majestic course just as it always has.

The Red Banks settlement has become the town of Henderson, Kentucky. Where Isaac and his boyhood friends crossed the river on the day of their capture, there is now a great span of stone and steel over which the roaring locomotives pass.

Chicagou, "the place that smells bad," where the black man, Jean Baptiste, had his tiny trading post, has become Chicago, the second largest city in the nation. Detroit and Cincinnati, likewise, have become great cities, and thriving towns now occupy the sites of Fort Defiance and Fort Greenville. A mighty bridge five miles long now spans the Straits of Mackinac.

What the man predicted that night in the Cafe Edmond in Detroit has, indeed, come true.

"The day is coming soon," he said, "and you can mark my word, when the Americans will take over all this country."

CPSIA information can be obtained at www.ICGtesting.com
Printed in the USA
LVOW03*0002250614

391484LV00027B/449/P